# *Living*
# *with*
# LUPUS

# *Living with*

# LUPUS

## *All the Knowledge You Need to Help Yourself*

Sheldon Paul Blau, M.D.
with Dodi Schultz

**Addison-Wesley Publishing Company**
Reading, Massachusetts   Menlo Park, California
New York   Don Mills, Ontario   Wokingham, England
Amsterdam   Bonn   Sydney   Singapore   Tokyo   Madrid
San Juan   Paris   Seoul   Milan   Mexico City   Taipei

Many of the designations used by manufacturers and sellers to distinguish their products are claimed as trademarks. Where those designations appear in this book and Addison-Wesley was aware of a trademark claim, the designations have been printed in initial capital letters.

This book is meant to educate and should not be used as an alternative to appropriate medical care. The author has exerted every effort to ensure that the information presented is accurate up to the time of publication. However, in light of ongoing research and the constant flow of information, it is possible that new findings may invalidate some of the data presented here.

The names of the people with lupus quoted in this book have been changed, as have certain other details, in order to protect their privacy. None are patients of the author.

*Library of Congress Cataloging-in-Publication Data*

Blau, Sheldon Paul, 1935–
   Living with lupus : all the knowledge you need to help yourself / Sheldon Paul Blau with Dodi Schultz.
        p. cm.
   Includes bibliographical references and index.
   ISBN 0-201-60809-X
1. Systemic lupus erythematosus—Popular works. I. Schultz, Dodi. II.
Title.
RC924.5.L85B555 1993
362.1'9677—dc20                                                          93-8896
                                                                              CIP

Cover design by Hannus Design Associates

Production services by Julianna Nielsen, Sloane Publications

Text design by Patty J. Topel

Set in Palatino 11-point by Patty J. Topel


3 4 5 6 7-DOH-97969594
Third printing, July 1994

To Bette, my best friend and my wife of thirty-six years

To Debra, a very special person who lights up my life

To Steven, who has always made me so very proud

To Brett, who should be a template for all sons-in-law

To Vicki, a woman of grace, elegance, and intelligence

To Butch, the best of all brothers

# Contents

Introduction ........................................................................................ 1

1. In Their Own Words: How It Began ................................... 9

2. Diagnosis: What Makes the Difference ........................... 19

3. Why Me?  What Causes Lupus—Maybe ......................... 37

4. Doctor and Patient: A Delicate Partnership ................. 59

5. Drugs Used for Lupus ........................................................ 73

6. The Main Medicines: Corticosteroids ............................. 85

7. Other Problems, Other Treatments ................................ 93

8. Osteoporosis: Detection and Prevention .................... 107

9. A Prudent Approach to Pregnancy ............................... 133

10. The "Other" Lupus: Drugs—and More—That Can Cause Disease ................................................................................ 149

11. Food Boosts, Cosmetic Cautions, and Other Practical Pointers ................................................................................ 165

12. The *Rest* of Your Life ....................................................... 185

13. Lupus in Children and Teens ........................................... 197

14. New Directions, Future Therapies ................................ 211

*Appendix:* Good Connections (You're Not Alone) ........................ 219

Glossary ........................................................................................... 231

Selected Bibliography ................................................................... 243

Index ................................................................................................ 253

About the Authors ......................................................................... 263

# Introduction

Lupus (its full medical name is systemic lupus erythematosus) is a mysterious illness. Although various aspects of it were described as far back as the 1840s and it was recognized as a systemic disease well over a century ago, the cause is still unknown and a cure still elusive.

Like AIDS (the letters stand for acquired immunodeficiency syndrome), lupus involves the immune system. There the similarity ends. Lupus is not transmissible from one individual to another; in no case has contagion even been suspected. In the majority of patients it does not prove fatal. And the illness is essentially the *opposite* of AIDS: The body's defenses don't falter or flag but become hyperactive, fiercely assaulting an individual's own tissues as if those tissues were offending intruders, foreign agents that must be destroyed or expelled. It is as if one has developed immunity to oneself, and lupus is classed as an *autoimmune* disease (the prefix "auto" means "self"); indeed, it is considered the prototype, the prime example, of such diseases.

Some other autoimmune conditions involve a single organ or system; diabetes mellitus and Graves' disease, affecting the pancreas and the thyroid gland, respectively, are among them. In lupus, the targeted tissues may be any from the skin to the joints to vital organs, and evidence of lupus activity may range from a bothersome rash to critical kidney dysfunction. Lupus runs the gamut from a persistent nuisance to a threat to life—in different people, or in the same person at different times. Lupus is a battle of the body against itself.

There is no cure, nothing that will vanquish the disease. Although there may be periods of remission when little or no treatment is necessary, lupus is chronic, a lifelong presence. But there are many effective ways of dealing with its manifestations, both its minor annoyances and its major complications.

It has been estimated that between five hundred thousand and one million Americans suffer from lupus. The numbers, however, may actually be higher. Lupus isn't an officially reportable condition, so there are no central tabulations such as are kept by the Centers for Disease Control and Prevention for AIDS, tuberculosis, measles, and so on. Estimates have therefore been based on other sources, mainly physician surveys.

One reason for the probable underestimate has been the inclination, until recently, not to count those patients whose symptoms are limited to the skin. For many years it was believed that theirs was a distinct disease, known as "discoid lupus" because of the appearance of the skin lesions, which are raised and roughly disk-shaped. It's now recognized that it is simply a part of the lupus spectrum.

Another reason may be an even more restrictive data base. A report at a recent meeting of the American College* of Rheumatology (the organization of physicians specializing in lupus, rheumatoid arthritis, and related diseases) suggested that the generally accepted estimates have relied chiefly on hospitalization data. Fewer than half of lupus patients followed by one researcher for almost a decade were ever hospitalized during that period, so most of those patients weren't part of the statistics. In my experience, and that of many other physicians, the hospitalization rate is even lower, about 10 to 15 percent. Thus, figures based on the assumption of higher hospitalization rates are likely to be gross underestimates of the overall prevalence of lupus.

At least eight out of nine lupus sufferers are women, most of them young at the time the disease strikes. Although lupus has been diagnosed in both small children and senior citizens, the concentration of cases (at the time of diagnosis) occurs during the teen years through the forties, with a mean onset age of twenty-nine or thirty. During these years of highest incidence, the female-to-male ratio is at least ten to one (after the mid-fifties, it drops to around two to one); we'll explore the possible reasons for these figures.

Lupus, as every lupus patient knows, is a frustrating experience. Your physician cannot explain its cause, predict its course, or promise a cure. This bafflement, this inability of medicine to clarify the nature and outcome of lupus, has led, as many medical mysteries do, to speculation, to theories, to a continuing

---

*"Colleges" and "academies" mentioned in connection with medical specialties are not institutions of higher learning but professional associations.

search for solutions. It has also led, at times, to the spreading of outrageous misinformation.

Until the 1970s, lupus was little known to the public and even to writers of popular home health guides. It's not surprising that some books published in the 1950s and 1960s characterized lupus as "rare," or as "a disease of the skin."

I think it *is* surprising, and disturbing, that, in 1988, a major U.S. health magazine published an article describing lupus as "an often-fatal degeneration of the nerves that's hard for physicians to diagnose" and stating that it "tends to run in families." If you, as a lupus patient—or as a member of a lupus patient's family—had seen that article, I can imagine how distressed you might have been.

Lupus *can* be difficult to diagnose, especially for an inexperienced or uninformed physician; that much is accurate. But I assure you that lupus is, in fact, *not* often fatal. Many examinations of survival rates in lupus patients have been published over the years—and those years have made a difference. A summary published in 1955 showed a five-year survival rate of only 50 percent. Another summary, published in 1964, reported a survival rate at five years of 69 percent, and at ten years of 54 percent (no ten-year figure was included in the 1955 report). Recently reported studies, conducted in the United States and in Europe in 1989–1991, have shown five-year survival to be 89 to 97 percent and ten-year survival from 83 to 93 percent.

The tremendous jump in these survival rates is, by the way, a little deceptive. Treatment of lupus is indeed far more effective today than it was in the 1950s, and the outlook for the patient is far rosier now than it was then. But diagnosis has also come a long way in these four decades. The 1955 survival rate of only 50 percent was doubtless based on only a fraction of those who actually had lupus, and those who were "counted" probably represented the most serious and complicated cases. Even today, many cases of lupus are still not diagnosed, so the most recently published survival rates are probably low.

Lupus is *not* a "degeneration of the nerves"; nor does it "run in families." (Not, at least, in the sense of being directly inherited, like hemophilia or cystic fibrosis. There *may* be a familial susceptibility, as well as shared exposure to environmental factors; I'll explore some of those factors in chapter 3.)

I'm especially disturbed by such misstatements as this because I know how depressing and frustrating the disease can sometimes be; someone who has it doesn't need further discouragement, particularly discouragement based on falsehood. Indeed, despite the fact that lupus can be neither surely prevented nor surely cured, there is much that *can* be done, by both you *and* your doctor, to control the disease, prevent complications, and ease the impact of lupus on your life.

If a crisis does occur, your physician can now summon sophisticated diagnostic and therapeutic technology to your aid, and the efficacy of that technology is increasing steadily. But chances are that will not happen to you; as I've said, as few as 10 to 15 percent of lupus patients are ever sick enough to need hospitalization.

Most lupus patients never face a major crisis; they simply cope, day to day, with what seems at times to be a succession of minor crises. Some of that coping can be aided by your physician, who can prescribe and suggest ways to ease discomfort and deal with the disease's vexingly unforeseeable course. Some is best done by you.

There are now new insights into lupus and its physical and emotional impact (those areas are, in lupus, uniquely linked). There is new thinking, and there are new therapies—not only medical treatment but alternative approaches a patient can successfully take on her own, both to relieve and to prevent problems.

In this book, I want to share those insights and that news with you, along with the latest medical research. I hope that if you have lupus, or someone you love has lupus, you'll gain new understanding of the condition—and, most important, a new appreciation of *living* with lupus.

## A Note on Names

Some readers may be puzzled by the name itself. Why is the disease called "lupus"? Before we go on to meet some of those who are living with lupus and explore what that means in the 1990s, here is a brief explanation.

*Lupus* is the Latin word for "wolf." It was first used in the mid-nineteenth century to denote a disease characterized by "malignant ulceration often destroying the nose, face, etc" (the definition in the first U.S. medical dictionary).[*]Someone probably thought the damage caused by the disease resembled the result of an attack by a ravenous wolf.

The full medical term for the disease described above, which is totally unrelated to the condition *now* called lupus, was *lupus vulgaris* (the latter Latin word simply means "common" or "ordinary"). That term is now obsolete, and the modern name is cutaneous tuberculosis. This form of TB results in extensive ulceration and tissue destruction and affects the face more

---

[*]C. H. Cleaveland, M.D. *Pronouncing Medical Lexicon, Containing the Correct Pronunciation and Definition of Most of the Terms Used by Speakers and Writers of Medicine and the Collateral Sciences.* Longley Brothers (Cincinnati), 1857.

often than other sites, especially around the nose and cheeks. (The tuberculosis bacterium typically targets the lungs, but it occasionally attacks other parts of the body.) In the 1850s, the infectious cause of the disease was unknown; the tuberculosis bacillus wasn't identified until 1882.

Some years before, in the 1840s, the Viennese physician Ferdinand von Hebra had described a distinctive rash—"mainly on the face, on the cheeks and nose in a distribution not dissimilar to a butterfly." This is, of course, the now-famous "butterfly rash," which is probably the best-known characteristic of lupus, although it appears in only a minority of cases. This is the first instance in the medical literature of a description of the condition we now know as lupus.

Clearly, this was not the destructive affliction then known as lupus vulgaris, although it seemed to affect the same area. Since it was a different condition, a different name was needed. In 1851, Pierre Cazenave combined the Latin word already in use with a coined, Greek-rooted French one and introduced the term *lupus erythemateux*—"lupus characterized by redness." The second word was soon Latinized to *erythematosus*. Later, after it had been conclusively demonstrated that the condition affects various parts of the body, "disseminated" was added up front; still later, that was changed to "systemic."

Now, patients and physicians alike refer to the disease simply as "lupus."

# 1

# In Their Own Words: How It Began

There are as many pictures, as many personal experiences, of lupus as there are people who have had it. Lupus is much like the elephant in an old folktale. Having heard of elephants but never having seen one, a curious monarch directed his wisest advisors to go forth, find and examine the exotic beast, and return and describe it. Unfortunately, all of the sages were sightless. Depending on whether each had encountered a leg, tusk, trunk, or tail, the animal was likened to a tree trunk, a spear, a serpent, or a rope.

The first experience with lupus is often recognized only in retrospect—seen at the time as something else or, often, simply an enigma. Only when lupus is finally suspected and diagnosed may it be clear that events that took place months or even years earlier were actually—or, at least, possibly—signs and symptoms of lupus, or that seemingly unrelated incidents may actually have been connected.

Here are brief introductions to a few people. All of them have lupus. Yet in no two instances did the disease start precisely the same way or follow exactly the same course. And none of them —indeed, *no* individual with lupus—can be called "typical."

## Anita

Anita, an Indiana homemaker now in her early fifties, was diagnosed only in her mid-forties after a bout of pleurisy. Now that she knows a good deal more about lupus, she says, "There was at least one other time that I had what I believe must have been symptoms of lupus. I think I was about thirty-eight or forty. I remember having really bad pains in my joints, just for a few days, with a rash on my cheeks—I'm pretty sure it was what they call the butterfly rash—and a little fever. I did go to the doctor, but the tests didn't show anything. And then it all went away." (More about that distinctive rash in the next chapter.)

Between that episode and the one that led to suspicion and diagnosis of lupus, and since her diagnosis, Anita has had no symptoms more serious than what she dismisses casually as "a few aches and pains." She takes no regular medication for lupus—only anti-inflammatory drugs prescribed by her physician when, from time to time, those aches and pains return.

## Connie

Connie's first clue to something amiss came in her late teens, with the onset of joint discomfort in her hands that wasn't disabling or even particularly painful but was persistent enough to send her to her family doctor in the small Pennsylvania town where she grew up. It was rheumatoid arthritis, she was told.

The aches returned from time to time, never severely enough to be truly worrisome.

Then, a decade later, in 1978—now married and living in a Boston suburb—Connie became pregnant, and there were "a *lot* of complications: I had thrombophlebitis, and pulmonary emboli, and my obstetrician said, 'I think you have a collagen disease.' I told my internist about that comment, but he dismissed the idea. And then, after my daughter was born, I had phlebitis in my legs. And oh, yes, a few years before, when I'd taken birth control pills, I had a strange negative reaction, with these huge lumps on my legs. I mentioned that to my internist, too, but—"

Connie's obstetrician warned her about possibly dire results should she attempt another pregnancy. She sought second and third opinions; all were in agreement, and she has followed their advice. There were no further episodes of circulatory problems. But a few years later, stretches of unexplained fatigue—and what she describes as "these weird blisters on the roof of my mouth"—posed new worries. She was still seeing the same obstetrician-gynecologist, who again had a helpful piece of advice: "He said, 'Why don't you see a rheumatologist?' So I finally did just that."

The "lumps" on Connie's legs may well have been symptoms of a condition called *erythema nodosum*, a form of vasculitis—blood-vessel inflammation—giving rise to painful reddish nodules, typically on the legs but occasionally on the arms or elsewhere. Although erythema nodosum is not peculiar to lupus patients, it does tend to strike people with lupus a little more often than people who do not have the disease. It may accompany a variety of infections, ranging from "strep" to tuberculosis to colitis, and may also occur in reaction to a number of drugs, notably sulfas and oral contraceptives.

To explain a term Connie mentioned: Her obstetrician suggested she might have a *collagen disease*. Collagen is a protein substance that forms an important part of connective tissue, both in the joints and throughout other parts of the body. "Collagen disease" was a term used to refer to those rheumatic disorders known to be systemic, affecting many tissues in the body—including lupus, progressive systemic sclerosis, dermatomyositis, and others—as distinguished from those, such as rheumatoid arthritis, impacting predominantly on the joints. The term has now largely fallen into disuse, and the conditions are now known collectively as connective-tissue diseases.

Connie also referred to phlebitis (venous inflammation) and thrombophlebitis (phlebitis with clot formation), as well as pulmonary emboli (fragments of such clots lodging in the lungs); see chapter 9 for more about lupus and pregnancy and the impact of each on the other.

## Eileen

Eileen was just twenty when she had a rather rude shock: "I had slept with exactly one person, and I was diagnosed as having syphilis in a routine screening test. In fact, I was *treated* for syphilis. I know now that was probably a false-positive test. Every once in a while, over the next ten years, I'd run low-grade fevers and feel kind of draggy, but my internist would say, 'Oh, it's just a virus; don't worry about it.'"

"Once," she recalls, "when I was about twenty-four—I was still living in Los Angeles, where I grew up [she's now an Oregonian]—one evening I was sitting in a movie theater, and my knees started to hurt. Later that night, I woke up and I couldn't move a single one of my joints; I had to call my parents to come across town and take me out of my apartment. I took a lot of aspirin, and it went away in about three days. Then it happened again a few days later. I'd been taking a sulfa drug for a bladder infection, and I finally realized I was allergic to it."

People with lupus do seem to have a higher prevalence of allergies—to drugs as well as other substances—than people in general. The sudden joint problem Eileen describes is medically termed *acute polyarthritis*—inflammation of many joints. It can be precipitated under many conditions, and hypersensitivity to sulfa is indeed one of them.

Interestingly, it was neither this symptom nor any other, but still another routine test, that led to Eileen's diagnosis of lupus. See the next chapter.

## Elizabeth

Elizabeth, an advertising copywriter who lives near Chicago, is now in her fifties and the mother of a grown son and daughter. She feels sure that her lupus was active as far back as twenty-some years ago: "I was extremely fatigued, running a fever every day. My then-internist kept saying he suspected lupus, and he had me in the hospital for tests. At first, everything came back negative. One of the specialists suggested it was all in my mind, that I was concerned about aging. I was thirty-one years old at the time! Finally, although they never did come up with a diagnosis, they found enough abnormal results to prove it wasn't psychosomatic."

"That was a relief," she says, "but it would have been a lot easier on me to know what it was. I was sick, even the specialists finally agreed with that, but I came out with no diagnosis. My rheumatologist says now that it wasn't their fault, that testing just wasn't as sophisticated then."

Not long afterward, Elizabeth had two operations, the second a hysterectomy: "In both cases, I had problems of postoperative hemorrhage. Then, for a dozen years, I had no problems whatever, until I had a minor fracture of my hand in 1984. It refused to heal."

Investigation of that refusal to heal was what led directly to Elizabeth's at-long-last diagnosis; see chapter 2.

## Jan

"Looking back," says Jan, who with her husband operates a computer-based design and promotion service in upstate New York, "I may have had a problem for years before it was diagnosed. I had a lot of things wrong from time to time, but I never connected them. The first thing I remember was a respiratory infection like none I'd ever had before. It went on for months. I went to three different doctors, all of whom concluded it was some kind of virus and none of whom could do anything about it. Eventually, it went away."

"Next," she recalls, "my feet started hurting. And there were changes in my menstrual patterns. My gynecologist said maybe it was early menopause—but I was only thirty-six. Then everything went back to normal—until I started getting wrist pains, which I figured had something to do with working at the computer. Then the foot pain came back, and then pain in my fingers. Then, my hair started to get thin, and I thought, well, I was forty by now, and my mother's hair has been thin for years, and I figured I was getting older. I decided that also accounted for the fact that the skin on my face was sort of dry and reddish. I was tiring very easily. And I was urinating very often—which could be a symptom of diabetes, except my husband, Charlie, has diabetes, and I tested myself with his glucose monitor, and it wasn't that."

"Well," she says, "my doctor didn't put these things together, either. I told him about the pain in my hands, and he said that often happened to women my age. About feeling tired, he said, 'You're no spring chicken.' He said I should talk to my gynecologist about the frequent urination, that it might be something called 'weak bladder syndrome.' I did, and my gynecologist said no, it wasn't. This was right before Thanksgiving, a very busy time for us, because clients are doing holiday promotions. And we had friends coming from out of town for Thanksgiving. Now, I am not the kind of person who normally lets anyone help out in the kitchen—but the pain in my fingers and wrists was so bad, I really needed help picking up pots and pans, and I was grateful for it."

As in Connie's case, it was another specialist who suggested the possibility of lupus to Jan: "I finally realized why I was going to the bathroom so often: My mouth was terribly dry all the time, and I'd gotten into the habit of keeping water, or juice, or a soft drink next to me all the time—next to my computer, and next to the bed at night—and I was drinking all these extra fluids, so of course I was having frequent urination. I'd also developed terrible gum problems. On my next visit to the dentist, he found some ulcers in my mouth—which I hadn't even been aware of, because they didn't hurt. I told him about my talk with my internist, and about some of my other problems. He said, 'I think you may have lupus.' He suggested I see a rheumatologist."

Jan's dry mouth may suggest a problem that plagues an estimated one in twenty of those with lupus, a condition known as Sjögren's syndrome; see page 175. For more about Jan's diagnosis, see chapter 2.

## Lisa

Lisa was in her mid-twenties, enjoying her job with a North Carolina landscaping firm and the fact that it took her outdoors in warm weather, when the first hint of lupus appeared. Unlike

Jan, with her constellation of symptoms, Lisa had only one complaint—a rash: "I saw a dermatologist. He just said I was allergic to the sun and advised me to use a sunscreen."

She did. But despite that precaution, the same thing happened the following spring: "I went to see a different dermatologist. He took one look at me and asked, 'Do you have lupus?' I said, 'What?' I had never *heard* of lupus. Then he asked me if I had any joint pains. And, well, I did; I just hadn't thought much about it. He sent me to a rheumatologist. The rheumatologist did blood tests, and he concluded that yes, I had lupus."

Lisa's first move was to visit her local library: "I took out an old medical book—very old, but it was the only one they had that mentioned lupus. It compared lupus to tuberculosis and said the life expectancy was three to seven years. I was very young, and I was very scared. Of course I know better now; it's been more inconvenient than life-threatening."

## Nancy

"I think it was about 1985," recalls Nancy, who sells real estate in Florida and was in her early thirties at the time. "I had a bout of arthritis. My internist referred me to a rheumatologist, who did some tests, but they didn't seem to tell much, and the arthritis went away by itself. I don't really know whether or not it had any connection with lupus. And I didn't have any other problems, for maybe four and a half or five years. Then, that winter, I had symptoms of Raynaud's; of course I didn't know what to call it, then, but my fingers would get cold and turn white. I was talking to a cousin who happens to be a doctor, and I mentioned it, and he said, you ought to see a rheumatologist."

Nancy returned to the specialist she'd consulted before, and that proved fortunate: "She'd done tests—which didn't show anything at all—when I saw her about the arthritis. But now, it was really helpful that she had a record of those normal, baseline values; she explained to me that there's a range of normal values for these things, and mine might be different from somebody else's. The new tests were positive, and they showed I have lupus. My doctor says that she isn't sure, but the arthritis a few years back could have been a kind of precursor of lupus, although she didn't feel I had lupus then."

You'll meet these patients again in later chapters; they've also been included in the index. In the very next chapter, let's look at how the diagnosis of lupus, with its confusing array of signs and symptoms, is made.

# 2

# Diagnosis: What Makes the Difference

How does a physician arrive at the conclusion that a patient is suffering from lupus? As noted, the diagnosis isn't an easy one, especially for a physician who is inexperienced. Many people visit three, four, or more doctors before lupus is either confirmed or eliminated from consideration.

I do feel the diagnosis should be made by a specialist, a rheumatologist, for a number of reasons, including familiarity with the spectrum of the disease (and related ills with which it can be easily confused) and awareness of the latest scientific information in the field. A primary-care physician, a general internist or family physician, who suspects the possibility of lupus will generally refer the patient to such a specialist.

Arriving at a diagnosis, even for the specialist, is still not a simple matter. A strep infection can be identified by the presence of bacteria in a test-tube culture; the diagnosis of diabetes may be made by measuring insulin responses. No such simple test exists for lupus. Rather, the physician's conclusions will be based on a combination of factors.

*The patient's complaints.* Lupus may begin with any one or more of a vast spectrum of symptoms, including—but not limited to—fever, fatigue, stomach upset, hair loss, and assorted aches and pains. Of course, all of these can be symptoms of many other conditions as well: allergic reactions, infections, and hormonal imbalances, to name just a few. There is, in particular, a great potential for overlap and confusion with other conditions in the "family" of which lupus is a part, generally known as the *connective-tissue disorders*, including rheumatoid arthritis, progressive systemic sclerosis (scleroderma), dermatomyositis, and polymyositis.

Sorting out the possibilities, a process known in medicine as *differential diagnosis*, is the challenge the physician faces. Depending on the individual patient's signs and symptoms, the physician may need to perform a number of tests to eliminate other diseases and disorders.

*Established diagnostic criteria.* These criteria were established by the Diagnostic and Therapeutic Criteria Committee of the American Rheumatism Association (ARA), then the medical arm of the Arthritis Foundation. (It became an independent professional organization in 1985 and later changed its name to the American College of Rheumatology.) I'll list those criteria—now known as the ACR criteria—shortly.

*Other factors.* The physician's experience frequently suggests other significant factors, beyond the official criteria. The official ACR criteria were based on surveys of leading rheumatologists in the United States and Canada. They were established in the early 1980s, replacing tentative criteria set up a decade earlier. The list may be further revised in the future as more reliable, more sensitive and, especially, more specific diagnostic tests are developed and reaffirmed. A brief explanation of two of those terms, which have been used here in a particular medical sense, is in order.

## Sensitivity and Specificity

Diagnostic testing relies on two concepts, *sensitivity* and *specificity*. The first word tells us whether or not a test is likely to miss many cases of the disease or disorder for which the patient is being tested. The second tells us whether or not the test is helpful in narrowing down the diagnosis to the condition being tested for.

Let's say, for example, that 90 percent of those with a condition we'll call "Dreaded Disease" have factor X in their blood. An accurate test for factor X would be positive in nine out of ten people with Dreaded Disease, "missing" only one in ten cases; it would be highly sensitive, thus useful for screening large populations.

But if factor X is also found in 40 percent of perfectly healthy people, or in 40 percent of those with an entirely different disease, a positive result would not really be very helpful in pinpointing true cases of Dreaded Disease. Thus, a test for factor X would be low in specificity—-not very useful for an individual patient's diagnosis.

Or, let's say there's another clue, called factor Y, that's found in 50 percent of those with Dreaded Disease but in only 1 percent of people who don't have the disease. An accurate test for factor Y could not be called sensitive, since it would miss half the cases of the disease—all those cases occurring in people with the disease but without factor Y. On the other hand, it would be far more specific than the test for factor X: A positive test for factor Y would mean 99-to-1 odds that the patient had Dreaded Disease.

Ideally, an accurate diagnostic test for a particular disease would be 100 percent sensitive and 100 percent specific: A negative test would be guaranteed assurance that the patient doesn't have the disease (since the test wouldn't miss any cases), and a positive test would tell the physician the patient definitely has the disease (and not some other disease, or no disease at all). No such test yet exists for lupus, for the simple reason that the testing would have to rely on a factor unique to lupus and present in all cases of the disease. No such factor has yet been found.

Therefore, a combination of judgments is needed for diagnosis.

## The ACR Diagnostic Criteria

Here are the American College of Rheumatology's eleven diagnostic criteria for lupus. Four are considered necessary to establish the diagnosis without question (the four needn't be present simultaneously). Some of the criteria are symptoms experienced by the patient or observable by both patient and physician; others must be determined by blood tests or other procedures.

It should be remembered that this list is an incomplete one, subject to future revision. Perhaps half of all those who have lupus will ever fully "qualify" (have four of the criteria) on the basis of the present criteria alone.

*Butterfly rash.* A reddish eruption across the bridge of the nose and winging out over the cheekbones, in a sort of butterfly configuration. As I noted in the introduction, it was this rash that, by a roundabout route, gave the disease its name. It is often cited as a classic symptom of lupus—probably more due to its picturesque name than its prevalence: It's an initial symptom in fewer than one in twenty cases of lupus, and only 40 to 50 percent of lupus patients (reported surveys have varied somewhat) will *ever* have it. The rash isn't itchy or particularly painful, although it may burn slightly, usually only on exposure to the sun; it eventually goes away and leaves no residual marking.

Some are clearly unacquainted with the rarity of the butterfly rash, especially as an early symptom of lupus. One patient, after reading one of my earlier books, wrote me to say that she had been dismissed by a physician who declared, "You can't possibly have lupus. You don't have the butterfly rash, and all those with lupus have the rash."

*Discoid lesions.* Reddish, raised patches, anywhere on the body, sometimes referred to as *discoid lupus erythematosus* (DLE), which used to be thought of as a disease distinct from *systemic lupus erythematosus* (SLE). DLE is now considered a part of the lupus spectrum. The lesions are roughly disk-shaped, thick, and scaly, and they may leave scars after healing.

This kind of skin lesion occurs in about 15 percent of lupus patients, and only 5 to 10 percent of those who have it also have involvement of other parts of the body. Some observers believe that part of the reason the number of those with lupus have been underestimated is that these patients have, by and large, been omitted.

*Photosensitivity of the skin.* It's specifically evidenced by a rash following exposure to sunlight. This was Lisa's very first symptom (see chapter 1). Although only about one-third of those with lupus are sun-sensitive, the reaction should suggest the possibility of lupus to any physician, as it did to the second dermatologist Lisa consulted.

*Ulcerative sores.* The sores, in the mouth or throat, are usually painless. These are the lesions Jan's dentist found. Sometimes, when they first arise, they are blister-like in appearance, as Connie described those she had on the roof of her mouth. About one in eight lupus patients have them at some time.

*Arthritis.* Joint inflammation—characterized by pain on motion, tenderness, and swelling—in two or more peripheral joints. (Peripheral joints are those of the hands, arms, feet and legs.) Joint aches, which are much like those of rheumatoid arthritis, are among the first symptoms in three of four cases of lupus, and at least 90 percent of patients will have arthralgia (joint pain) or arthritis sooner or later. The earliest arthritis symptom (in both lupus and rheumatoid arthritis) is usually morning stiffness of the fingers and wrists.

The severity of the arthritis can vary considerably. Lisa's chronic discomfort, you'll recall, was so slight that she "hadn't thought much about it" until the subject was raised by her physician.

Although Jan's dentist advised her to see a rheumatologist, she didn't do so immediately. But her joint pain soon became overpowering: "I'd been taking ibuprofen—not in the doses on the label, but in enormous quantities. Sometimes it seemed to help, and sometimes it didn't; it was a coming-and-going situation."

"Then," she continues, "one weekend—this was now early spring—Charlie and I went on a trip to a country inn, one of our favorite getaways. Our first full day, we did what we like to do most on these trips—lots of walking. The next morning, I had extreme pain in my feet and legs. The pain stayed bad during the following week. A few days later, I wound up lying on the bed all night, crying, with Charlie putting ice packs on every joint. In the morning, I called the rheumatologist and announced that I was in serious pain. She saw me right away."

And Jan found out that her dentist's suspicion was right. "I had a sense of relief, almost elation, at having a diagnosis. I'm not crazy. I'm not lazy. It has a name. Charlie's reaction was a little different; he said, 'Oh, God. Flannery O'Connor.'* I explained that I wasn't going to die of it. But my own attitude was unrealistic, too, and I didn't know as much as I thought I did. I figured, yes, I understand it's chronic, but we'll just spend a couple of years finding the right drug program, and then I'll feel perfectly normal again. Well, now I know that I won't."

**Chest/heart problems.** Evidence of either pleuritis (inflammation of the pleura, the membrane lining the chest cavity) or pericarditis (inflammation of the pericardium, the outer membrane surrounding the heart). The patient has usually complained of chest pain, and the physician will order a chest X ray and electrocardiogram (ECG) to investigate.

It was pleuritis—more popularly called "pleurisy"—that led to Anita's diagnosis: "I had what seemed to be flu, then it became bronchitis and pneumonia, then it became pleurisy. I was referred to a lung specialist, who put me in the hospital. He, in turn, called in a rheumatologist," who confirmed what the pulmonary specialist suspected.

---

*Flannery O'Connor is probably the most renowned name associated with lupus, from which the gifted short-story writer and novelist died in 1964, at the age of thirty-nine; she had first become ill in her mid-twenties. A collection of her letters, *The Habit of Being*, chronicling her life, her work, and her feelings about her illness, was published in 1980.

As Anita says, "There isn't one test that says, yes, you absolutely have lupus. You kind of back into it."

Various studies have shown that one-third to approximately 45 percent of those with lupus have pleurisy at one time or another, though not necessarily initially, and about 25 percent will experience pericarditis.

*Renal (kidney) disorder.* Kidney problems may be suggested by a persistent high level of proteinuria, the presence of certain proteins in the urine, or by discovery in the urine of elements known as cellular casts, which are fragments of bodily substances not normally found in the urine, such as hemoglobin. Urinalysis is a standard part of the differential diagnosis, since it can also reveal other conditions such as diabetes and urinary-tract infections. Perhaps half of all lupus patients will have some degree of kidney involvement at some time.

*Signs of neurologic disorder.* Seizures or psychosis, occurring without explanation. Other causes may include toxic drugs, injury, and metabolic derangement; infection is also a possible cause of sudden seizures. If there are such symptoms, diagnostic procedures may include an electroencephalogram (EEG) and a lumbar puncture ("spinal tap") to obtain a sample of the cerebrospinal fluid that bathes the brain and flows down through the spinal canal. Such disorders affect a small but significant proportion of those with lupus, perhaps 15 percent.

*Hematologic (blood) abnormalities.* These may include hemolytic anemia (caused by too-rapid destruction of red blood cells), leukopenia (a deficit in white cells), or thrombocytopenia (a deficit in thrombocytes or platelets, the clotting cells); a symptom of the last may be "bruises" in the absence of injury, caused by spontaneous bleeding of small vessels in the skin. A complete blood count (CBC) is, of course, a basic diagnostic procedure. Just about all lupus patients will have some hematologic departure from the norm at some point, though not necessarily at the time of diagnosis.

You'll remember that Elizabeth's complaints of fever and fatigue didn't lead to a diagnosis and that later she experienced postoperative hemorrhaging following two surgical procedures. Still later, in a fall on an icy sidewalk, she suffered a hairline fracture of a wrist bone. It refused to heal, and her worried doctors discovered that she'd been having wrist-to-elbow internal hemorrhaging, a clear signal of thrombocytopenia. Further blood tests confirmed the diagnosis of lupus.

*Immunologic disruption.* Such disruption is suggested by any of the following four findings in blood tests:

1. A false-positive reaction to the standard test for syphilis, persisting for at least six months and confirmed as false by the use of alternative testing methods.* (You remember that Eileen had what she now believes was a false-positive syphilis test. She was not given any alternative tests.) This occurs in about 20 percent of those with lupus.

2. A positive LE-cell test (sometimes referred to as "LE prep"), a test for a unique sort of white cell that shows evidence of a phenomenon called aberrant phagocytosis. Certain white cells normally practice phagocytosis, roughly translatable

---

*"False-positive" suggests falsely that the patient has the disease being tested for. The false-positive suggestion of syphilis (which can also occur in other conditions, including acute hepatitis) is associated with a widely used screening test called the RPR (for rapid plasma reagin). Two other tests—the FTA-ABS (for fluorescent treponemal antibody absorption) or the TPI (for *Treponema pallidum* immobilization)—may be used to rule out syphilis.

as "cell-eating," in which bacteria, body discards, and other cellular debris are disposed of; the LE cell is such a cell detected in the process of devouring nuclear core material from another white cell, after the latter has been attacked by a destructive agent called antideoxyribonucleoprotein antibody.

LE cells are found in an estimated 40 to 50 percent of lupus patients at one time or another, especially when the disease is active (lupus has a flare-and-subside pattern). Despite their name, however, LE cells aren't unique to lupus; the test is also positive in 5 to 10 percent of those with rheumatoid arthritis. Some common medications can also cause a positive LE-cell test in some people.

3. An abnormal (heightened) level of anti-DNA, an antibody to DNA (deoxyribonucleic acid), in particular, double-stranded DNA (dsDNA), or "native" DNA, the kind found within the nucleus of all human cells; this antibody is often denoted "anti-dsDNA." Anti-dsDNA is found in 50 to 60 percent of lupus patients at some time. Some researchers believe that antibody to native DNA may be unique to lupus.

DNA with another molecular structure, known as single-stranded DNA (ssDNA), is also found in the bloodstream as a result of the normal breakdown of old or damaged cells. Most lupus patients also have anti-ssDNA, but so do many of those with rheumatoid arthritis and other connective-tissue disorders.

4. The presence of anti-Sm, another antibody. Sm is not a medical abbreviation but stands for the name of the patient in whom it was first identified; it is a nuclear protein. Anti-Sm has been found in fewer than half of lupus patients but, like anti-dsDNA, it may be specific for lupus.

*ANA, short for antinuclear antibodies.* These are antibodies that act indiscriminately against material from cell nuclei. They don't actually invade cells but, rather, apparently react to a variety of proteins that may be released when cells have been destroyed.

High ANA levels are highly suggestive of lupus, though not exclusive to lupus; they're also found in a number of other conditions including rheumatoid arthritis and liver disease, and in some infections, as well as in those taking certain medications. The proportions of positive results vary, however, from close to 100 percent of lupus patients to about 30 percent of people with rheumatoid arthritis. Proportions also vary among those with other connective-tissue disorders and other diseases. A small percentage of perfectly healthy elderly people also test positive. ANA testing is thus highly sensitive, but not specific.

The last two ACR criteria mention *antibodies*. The reader may be more familiar with the word in connection with infectious diseases, where antibodies are viewed as highly desirable. They are developed by the body in response to infection, or to a vaccination in which infectious agents are deliberately introduced to evoke the manufacture of antibodies. Thereafter, those antibodies stand guard, ready to defend the body against that particular disease-causing agent. A substance that provokes the body's immune system to produce antibodies is called an *antigen,* since it stimulates production of an "anti" substance; antigens are usually composed of protein.

But in lupus, and in the other connective-tissue disorders, tissues of the patient's own body are somehow perceived as foreign invaders, like bacteria or viruses, and *they* act as antigens. ANA and the other antibodies mentioned in the diagnostic criteria, unlike our antibodies against polio, measles, or the flu (for example), have been produced to do battle with the stuff of the body's own cells; they are *auto*(self)antibodies. Hence, the characterization of lupus and the others as *auto-immune* disorders—conditions in which the body is primed to protect itself against itself.

## Other Signs, Symptoms, and Tests

While they are not—at least, not *yet*—on the list of official criteria, there are a number of other signs, symptoms, and test results that, if present with others, will lead an experienced specialist to consider the possibility that a patient may have lupus. Some are considered more significant than others. Among them (the first two were included in the earlier, 1970s criteria but were later dropped):

*Hair loss.* Rapidly occurring, unexplained loss of hair from the scalp. There are many possible causes of hair loss, ranging from mechanical stress to allergies and infections, and the physician will, of course, look for such explanations. Jan, who experienced a wide range of symptoms, counted hair loss among them. About a quarter of all lupus patients experience some degree of hair loss.

*Raynaud's phenomenon.* Marked paling and numbing of the fingers—occasionally, the toes. It was an episode of Raynaud's, you'll recall, that sent Nancy to the consultation that led to her diagnosis. It can also occur alone, not in association with lupus or any other disorder. It is then known as Raynaud's *disease* or Raynaud's *syndrome.*

This condition, caused by vasospasm, spasm of small blood vessels which cuts off circulation (cause unknown), is essentially identical to frostbite, although such extreme weather isn't needed for it to occur; attacks, lasting minutes or hours, may be triggered by cold but also by other stimuli, including emotional stress. Often, it's identified by color as the "red, white, and blue" phenomenon: The fingers or toes turn very pale, then blue, and these two stages are either preceded or, more often, followed by painful redness. Estimates of the number of persons with lupus who suffer from Raynaud's have varied from under 20 percent to 40 percent.

*Free DNA.* As noted, the antibodies in lupus are produced in response to encounters with the nuclear material of cells or specific components of that material. Unusually high levels of freely circulating DNA, which suggest high levels of cell destruction, while not specifically pointing to lupus, are highly suggestive of lupus.

*High sedimentation rate.* The erythrocyte (red blood cell) sedimentation rate (ESR; often called the "sed rate") denotes the sinking velocity of red cells within a quantity of drawn blood. The ESR is elevated in most lupus patients with active disease, in most rheumatoid arthritis patients, and during the course of many infections. A higher-than-normal ESR doesn't necessarily signify lupus, but it does indicate *something* amiss.

*Other antibodies.* One of the possibilities mentioned in the ACR diagnostic criteria was an antibody against a substance called Sm. Sm is one of several such substances, collectively called extractable nuclear antigens, or ENAs; others include

Ro, La (like Sm, named for the patients in whom they were first discovered), and nRNP (nuclear ribonucleoprotein).* The specialist who suspects that a patient may have lupus will probably test for antibodies to all known ENAs.

About 15 percent and 30 percent of lupus patients have antibodies to La and Ro, respectively, often in combination with anti-Sm. An estimated 40 to 45 percent have anti-nRNP antibodies, which seem to be associated particularly with such symptoms as arthritis and Raynaud's phenomenon and with a low incidence of kidney involvement.

The newest class of antibodies to be recognized as relevant to lupus are the anti-phospholipids, and we now realize that a clue to their presence is the false-positive syphilis test, which Eileen believes she had at age twenty. A decade later, still symptomless except for the episode of acute arthritis she experienced at twenty-four, she had minor surgery, which was preceded by routine preoperative blood tests.

The results were disturbing: "The circulating anticoagulant came back positive. They were concerned to make sure I didn't have a clotting problem. They decided it was okay to go ahead with the surgery, but they warned me that I should consult a rheumatologist. I did, and I then went through a gamut of tests, which came back positive." Still, Eileen was to have no further symptoms for another five years. In spite of the clearly positive blood tests, she was enjoying an extended remission.

---

*Ro is also sometimes known as SS-A and La as SS-B, the designations they were given when first found, in patients with the condition called Sjögren's syndrome, which may exist alone and also affects some lupus patients. A person may have antibodies to Ro or La without having Sjögren's, however, so the Ro and La appellations are preferable.

The routine test that turned up the disquieting possibility of "a clotting problem" was one called the PTT, for partial thromboplastin time, and the substance revealed was an anti-phospholipid. Despite the word "anticoagulant," which seems to suggest it prevents blood clotting, it's actually associated with an increased formation of dangerously obstructive blood clots. Because the anti-phospholipids have proved to be a particularly vexing concern vis-à-vis pregnancy, I've discussed them in more detail later; see chapter 9.

*Serum complement.* The complement system, which is part of the body's overall defense operation, is a series of proteins that act as "backup" for the activity of antibodies. When antibodies attack antigens, they lock in combat (imagine two tenacious wrestlers), forming entities called immune complexes, which cause local inflammation and a certain amount of tissue damage. Immune complexes attract the complement-system components, which move in to destroy the membranes of the "enemy" cells by a number of techniques, including summoning phagocytes to the area, coating cell walls with a substance phagocytes can "recognize," and producing solvents to destroy the membranes.

The total amount of complement in the body at any given moment is finite. Thus, if complement has been drawn to sites of immune complex activity, there will be lower-than-normal levels in the general circulation. In lupus, at least in active disease, serum levels are low. (That fact can also prove helpful in monitoring treatment.)

*Rheumatoid factor.* A procedure called a latex fixation test may reveal a particular antibody, called rheumatoid factor, found in 75 to 80 percent of rheumatoid arthritis patients. The test is also positive in about 15 percent of lupus patients, as well as in 25 to 40 percent of those with scleroderma or polymyositis—that is, it is not highly specific, but it does signal connective-tissue disease of some sort.

*False-positive AIDS test.* In a few instances, false-positive tests for infection with the human immunodeficiency virus (HIV), the cause of acquired immunodeficiency syndrome (AIDS), have occurred in individuals who later turned out not to have AIDS but to have lupus.

The commonly used HIV screening test, because it is inexpensive and easy to perform, is the enzyme-linked immunosorbent assay, or ELISA; although the test is quite sensitive, it is not very specific, and false-positive results with ELISA are not uncommon. Other, more specific tests are available, notably the Western blot test—which is more costly and requires more expertise but should be used to confirm doubtful positive results on ELISA testing. Sometimes, even that precaution may not be completely dependable: In late 1992, a team of Venezuelan rheumatologists reported a case in which the Western blot test was also weakly positive in a patient with lupus and without AIDS (both tests were negative six months later). In early 1993, another such case was reported in a New York lupus patient being evaluated for kidney transplant; two other tests, polymerase chain reaction and viral culture, proved the earlier tests to be falsely positive.

## Sorting It Out

In medicine's past, syphilis was known as "the great imitator," because in its various stages it can affect many parts of the body and appear in many different and seemingly unrelated guises. Syphilis is, of course, now treated immediately, in its earliest stage, with antibiotics. Lupus has now assumed the "great imitator" title. As I've said, arriving at a definite diagnosis isn't easy, even with the use of laboratory tests, since there is significant "overlap" with other chronic disorders. Lupus may even be confused, in the short term, with *acute* ills.

One condition that might be singled out in this connection is a common, garden-variety childhood infection popularly known as "fifth disease" and technically termed *erythema infectiosum*. (The reason for the "fifth disease" designation is now lost to history: Presumably it stemmed from its position on a list of childhood ills accompanied by rashes—measles, chickenpox, and so on.) Erythema infectiosum is caused by a virus called parvovirus B19.

The chief symptom of fifth disease is a red rash which first appears on the cheeks, then comes and goes on other parts of the body over a period of two or three weeks; there may also be mild flu-like malaise. In adults—the incidence is especially high in parents, health professionals, teachers, and others who have close contact with children—the symptoms may include joint pain and fever, and the picture may bear an uncanny resemblance to lupus; there may even be positive results on ANA testing. Erythema infectiosum, though, will vanish in fairly short order.

Most experienced rheumatologists, when considering differential diagnosis, will first move quickly to eliminate those possibilities that are most serious and most likely to require prompt treatment—malignancies, serious infections, and dysfunctions of major organs. After that, if the diagnosis is in doubt and the patient isn't acutely ill, the best course may be to wait and see what happens next, not looking for anything specific, rather than rush to judgment or treatment.

Before we survey the treatment of lupus, let's look, in the next chapter, at its possible causes.

# CHAPTER

# 3

# Why Me? What Causes Lupus—Maybe

There is one kind of lupus—I've chosen to call it *lupus-like syndrome,* to avoid confusion with "regular" lupus—that departs when certain drugs or other agents are withdrawn. You'll find the syndrome discussed in chapter 10. Except for that syndrome, the cause of lupus is unknown—although there have been hints and suspicions.

But before we talk about what *may* cause lupus, let's take a look at what definitely *doesn't.*

In the late 1970s, a nasty slur made its way around the country, via a newsletter distributed to health-care institutions. The newsletter alleged that lupus was a fast-increasing disease, "mostly because of more permissive sexual mores," since it was "generally if not always transmitted by intercourse." It recommended that hospitals "get into the act" by sponsoring lupus clinics, which it suggested would not only constitute useful public relations but would also prove "potentially profitable."

As I've stated in no uncertain terms, lupus is not transmissible, by sexual intercourse or any other means. While there may be an infectious agent or agents involved in lupus, it is not an agent that can carry the condition from one person to another, like the measles virus or the bacteria that cause tuberculosis or syphilis. (Were the newsletter writers confusing lupus with AIDS, which would have fit their description? No; the first case of AIDS wasn't reported until several years later.)

Happily, there have not been any such erroneous statements issued in recent years, so far as I'm aware.

I don't know what *does* cause lupus; no one does, yet. But there are intriguing associations that seem to suggest, if not a cause, at least some sort of influence. Some current thinking holds that these factors may somehow interact to cause lupus, that two or even more must occur simultaneously. There are a number of interesting areas of study.

## The Genetic Connection

Jan has a sister who also has lupus, albeit a much milder case. And they suspect they're not the only ones in the family. "My sister and I think our mother [who is now in her late seventies] may have had it," Jan says. "We remember that when she was in her forties, she had a real bad time; she'd be exhausted, she'd have aches and pains and headaches. Nothing was ever diagnosed. I gather that years ago, lupus never got diagnosed unless there was a butterfly rash and kidney disease."

Jan's mother may or may not have had lupus, but it's probably true that most cases of lupus then went undiagnosed.

In the introduction, I dismissed the sweeping statement that lupus "tends to run in families," like cystic fibrosis or hemophilia, because it simply doesn't. There are very definite patterns for these and other directly heritable diseases, and the odds of passing them along to one's offspring can be mathematically calculated; depending on the mode of inheritance, the probabilities range from 25 to 100 percent.

That is not remotely true of lupus; there is only a 5 percent chance of a person with lupus having a child who will eventually develop lupus. Yet there are suggestions of more subtle genetic factors.

Overall, about 20 percent of lupus patients have a first-degree relative (parent, child, or sibling) with *some* autoimmune disorder, which might be lupus but might also be thyroid disease, insulin-dependent diabetes, rheumatoid arthritis, multiple sclerosis, or any of a number of other, less well known conditions. An additional 15 to 20 percent of lupus patients' close relatives, if their blood were thoroughly tested, would be found to have signs of immunologic aberration, such as antinuclear antibodies (ANA), although they have (and will have) no autoimmune disease.

Take, then, the question of twin concordance. Twins who share a characteristic are said to be *concordant* for that trait; if one has it and the other does not, they are *discordant* for it. In fraternal twins, who are *dizygotic* (originating from two separate fertilized egg cells) and are no more closely related than any two siblings of different ages, the likelihood that they will be concordant for lupus is a mere 3 to 5 percent.

But in identical (*monozygotic*) twins, who originated from a single fertilized egg cell and are genetically identical as well as look-alikes, much higher concordance has been reported, ranging in various studies from 22 to 70 percent. That's impressive and certainly suggests that some hereditary factor is at work.

But the figure is not 100 percent. Clearly, having an identical twin with lupus doesn't mean that you will have lupus, and there is not a single "lupus gene." Lupus is certainly not an inherited disorder in the traditional sense. Rather, the high degree of identical twin concordance suggests an inherited *susceptibility*; some additional factor(s) must be present, as well, for lupus to occur.

Another aspect of genetic study is what has come to be known as the HLA system. The letters stand for "human leukocyte antigen," because it was first found in leukocytes (white blood cells); the HLA region actually resides on the sixth chromosome of every human cell. It controls a number of immunological responses, including the acceptance or rejection of transplanted tissue and organs. (It is also known as the MHC, for "major histocompatibility complex"; *histos* is Greek for "tissue.")

As scientists have studied this tiny but influential territory, they have pinpointed a variety of subregions—designated A, B, C, and so on—and, within those subregions, certain proteins that have been determined to be genetic "markers"; like blood types, they are determined by heredity. HLA "typing" is now standard procedure in transplant surgery.

But these HLA markers indicate more than whether or not a person is likely to be compatible with another individual's kidney. The HLA region can apparently also reveal something about susceptibility to certain disorders.

The first such connection surfaced in the early 1970s, when researchers found that the HLA marker designated B27 turned up in 80 percent of those with ankylosing spondylitis, a disabling form of spinal arthritis which strikes mostly men and had been observed to recur in families. It was found in fewer than 10 percent of persons without the disease—and those who have B27 but are well may in fact be at high risk of being struck by spondylitis at some future time.

Since then, other HLA factors, especially those in the "D" subregion, have been associated with a variety of chronic health problems. DR4, for example, has been linked with both rheumatoid arthritis and diabetes and is found in almost *all* diabetics who also have severe periodontitis (disease of the supporting structures of the teeth). And two closely associated DR markers have been found in lupus patients in statistically significant numbers.

While results of various studies have not been completely consistent, DR3 has been found in 44 to 54 percent of those who have lupus, versus only 20 to 36 percent of those who do not; DR2 has been found in more than half of lupus patients but in only about a quarter, or even fewer, of other individuals (DR2 has also been linked to multiple sclerosis). Overall, 75 to 85 percent of lupus patients have either DR2, DR3, or both; that's true for fewer than half of other people. Among the 30 percent of lupus patients who have anti-Ro antibodies (see page 32), at least one of the two markers has been found in a whopping 96 percent.

Most recently, the "next-door" DQ subregion has been found even more closely associated with a number of the specific antibodies I mentioned in chapter 2. Those associations include DQ2, DQ6, or DQ8 with anti-DNA; DQ5 or DQ8 with anti-nRNP; and a DQ6 subtype with anti-Sm (there's also an association of this antibody with DR4 and DR7). Lupus patients who have both DQ2 and DQ6 almost always have both anti-La and anti-Ro antibodies (and those with these two antibodies, interestingly, nearly always have DR4 as well). And DQ7 is linked with anti-phospholipid antibodies. (These antibodies, which have significant implications in pregnancy and childbirth, are discussed in chapter 9.)

These associations are not important only in the search for causes of lupus and other conditions. They may have significance for prevention as well. If environmental, infectious, or other "triggers" of disease are found, for example, it may be possible to take selective steps to protect those who, while not ill, are genetically susceptible to the disorder or to particular complications of it.

Still another suggestion of a genetic component in lupus lies in its racial distribution. While lupus is doubtless under-reported and firm figures are hard to come by, it's been estimated that lupus strikes one in 700 women between the ages of twenty and sixty-four. But among African-American women in the same age group, the incidence is estimated to be about one in 245, nearly three times as high. Lupus is also more prevalent among both Asians and Native Americans than among whites, and some observers have noted higher prevalence among Hispanics. Changing demographics of the U.S. population may mean a notable increase in the prevalence of lupus.

## Sex Discrimination

The fact that lupus strikes at least eight or nine times as many women as men might seem to suggest another hereditary linkage—something like the reverse of the situation in the recessive X-linked disorders.

Each fertilized egg cell contains twenty-three pairs of chromosomes; one of those pairs are the sex chromosomes—two X chromosomes for females, an X and a Y for males. Genes for many hereditary conditions—ranging from red-green color-blindness to hemophilia and a type of muscular dystrophy—are carried on the X chromosome but are recessive to (a genetics term meaning that they defer to) opposite information on another X chromosome. An XX person, a female, with at least one "healthy" X chromosome, is thus protected—while in an XY person, a male, the gene for the disease is unopposed. Thus, a woman can be an unaffected "carrier" and can pass on a disorder to her sons.

But as we've said, no "lupus gene" has ever been found, despite long and diligent searching, and the possibility that genetic information on the Y chromosome "protects" most men from lupus is unlikely.

It's well known that coronary heart disease strikes more men than women—until menopause. After the childbearing years, women are equally susceptible, unless they have been given replacement therapy to counter the postmenopausal depletion in certain hormones, predominently the kind called estrogens. It is not an anti-heart-disease gene that protects most women for most of their lives but, very likely, estrogen.

With lupus, the prevalence picture is precisely the opposite. Lupus has been diagnosed in infants and nonagenarians, but the concentration of cases at onset is from the teens to the forties; during these years, the ratio of females to males among lupus patients may be as much as fifteen to one, and some estimates have even run as high as thirty to one. After the age of about fifty-five, the ratio drops to approximately two to one. A study of all the children and teenagers diagnosed with lupus over more than a decade at a major metropolitan children's hospital showed a dramatic spurt in new cases at ages eleven and twelve, the onset of puberty.

Might the hormones that probably protect women from heart disease play a role in promoting lupus? If so, might one expect to find unusual departures from normal hormone profiles in people with lupus? These questions have been studied, but the number of research subjects has been small and the findings inconclusive, with both higher- and lower-than-average levels of androgens ("male" hormones) and estrogens ("female" hormones) found in both men and women (both sexes produce both; it's proportion that counts).

There is a race of hybrid mice, known as NZB / NZW (they're native to New Zealand, and the line was developed by breeding black mice with white ones), that spontaneously develop an ailment striking in its resemblance to lupus in humans. They have been under study for more than three decades. In these mice, administration of estrogens has been found to accelerate the illness, and androgens have proved protective.

Some have suggested that the apparent significance of sex hormones in humans might be explained not by under- or oversupply but by how they're handled by the body. Disease due to lack of a vitamin isn't always due to *dietary* deficiency; sometimes, it's caused by inability to absorb or metabolize foods containing the nutrient. Many cases of diabetes are caused not by underproduction of insulin but by failure to utilize it properly.

Indeed, one small study did find that lupus patients of both sexes metabolized (chemically broke down) estradiol, an estrogen, differently from a group of healthy volunteers. And another small study recently reported by rheumatologists in Russia and France found increased activity in lupus patients (both male and female), compared to control subjects, of aromatase, an enzyme that converts circulating androgens to estrogens. Aromatase activity was especially elevated in patients with minimal disease activity; in those who were severely ill, aromatase levels decreased and were even lower than those in the healthy controls. The researchers weren't sure of the meaning of these findings.

How about the pattern of disease? Is lupus manifested differently in men and women? Not markedly, but one study reported in late 1992 did turn up some minor variations. Among 64 percent of the women, almost two-thirds, arthritis was an early symptom; that was true for only 40 percent of the men. The men, on the other hand, were more likely than the women to have discoid lesions at the onset of the disease (17 percent versus only 1 percent).

Later on (the patients were followed for an average of four and a half years), the men continued to be more likely than the women to have discoid lesions (20 percent versus 3 percent), while the women were more likely than the men to have arthritis (81 percent versus 60 percent) as well as the classic butterfly rash (52 percent versus 23 percent).

On the other hand, it must be noted that a second study, reported at about the same time, came up with no significant differences in symptoms between male and female patients. (The first study took place in Barcelona, the second in London. The numbers of patients were similar.)

## Pulling the Trigger: A Virus?

There must be some other factor or factors, though. If one thirty-five-year-old woman has lupus and her identical twin—with exactly the same genetic risk factors—does not, we have to conclude that the lupus patient has yet another risk factor, one that her twin does not. Logically, that must be something in her environment, something she has encountered that her sister has not. What might that be? Increasingly, the environmental factors that have come under strongest suspicion have been viruses in general, and certain categories of viruses in particular.

Viruses are organisms consisting of a core of genetic material surrounded by a protein coat or shell. All viruses are classed generally as either deoxyviruses or riboviruses, depending on whether their cores consist of deoxyribonucleic acid (DNA) or ribonucleic acid (RNA). Each class includes a number of subgroups.

Among the DNA viruses are the herpesviruses (herpes simplex types 1 and 2; varicella-zoster virus, which causes chickenpox and shingles; cytomegalovirus; Epstein-Barr virus; and the recently recognized human herpesvirus 6—HHV-6—which causes roseola), the poxviruses (smallpox and others), and the large family of adenoviruses, which are responsible for many childhood nose, throat, and eye infections. (With the years, we build up some immunities.)

Most of these have been cleared of any connection with lupus. The exception is HHV-6. Researchers reported, at a 1992 international conference on lupus, a study in which a group of lupus patients, a group with rheumatoid arthritis, and a third group without autoimmune disease were tested for HHV-6 infection. They found active infection in 44 percent of the lupus patients but in only 2.3 percent and 6 percent, respectively, of the other two groups.

Among the RNA viruses are the myxoviruses, which have a special affinity for mucous membrane (*myxa* is Greek for "mucus") and include the flu viruses; the related paramyxoviruses, which include the measles, mumps, and rubella viruses; the parainfluenza viruses, which typically cause colds in adults but more serious respiratory ills in infants; and the reoviruses, which are not known—yet—to cause any specific diseases. (They've been associated with minor ills such as mild gastrointestinal upsets, but no cause-and-effect relationship has been proved.)

Remember that antibodies are produced by the body only in response to antigens; if antibodies are present, the body must have encountered the agent setting that production in motion.

In the case of a virus, the encounter may have involved either the virus itself or a component part of the virus.

Over the years, a number of RNA viruses have been tapped as possible culprits, or at least aiders and abetters, in lupus. Quite a few researchers have reported significant proportions of lupus patients with antibodies to reoviruses; in one study, the figure was 55 percent, versus only 3 percent of controls. Some have found comparatively high levels of antibodies to various parainfluenza viruses (there are four known strains) among those with lupus. Many have linked lupus to high levels of antibodies to the paramyxoviruses, especially the measles virus.

Most recently, there has been growing attention paid to still another subclass of RNA viruses, known as retroviruses. Not very much is understood yet about the retroviruses. Only in recent years have specific retroviruses been identified as responsible for human ills.

All viruses are essentially parasites: They must invade living tissue in order to thrive and multiply. The viral particle, called a virion, penetrates a target cell, where it releases its core material (DNA or RNA) and proceeds to loot the host cell. Using the mechanisms that cell would normally use to produce its own proteins to manufacture proteins and nucleic acids, it produces new viral particles, each a clone of the original. The new virions then go on to ravage other cells.

This dependence on cell invasion is one of the means by which viruses elude the usual antibiotics, which can easily seek out and destroy bacteria wandering the bloodstream. Antiviral drugs, thus far few in number, must rely on more sophisticated strategies that will vanquish infectious agents while sparing the host itself, typically by interfering in some way with the virus's reproductive process.

A retrovirus carries an effective weapon, an enzyme called reverse transcriptase, which enables it to convert its RNA to DNA and then slip into the target cell virtually undetected. There it may remain for a long time, even years, until some unknown signal activates it.

It had been known for some time that retroviruses were responsible for a number of kinds of malignancies in animals. It was not until 1981 that a retrovirus was found to cause a human illness, a rare form of leukemia; it was dubbed HTLV, for human T-cell lymphotropic virus.

To explain those terms: "Lymphotropic" denotes its attraction to the subgroup of white blood cells called lymphocytes, essentially the front line troops of the body's defense system. They, in turn, are divided into T-cells (for "thymus-dependent") and B-cells (for "bone-marrow-dependent"). The B-cells produce immunoglobulins containing antigen-specific antibodies. The T-cells, on encounter with a virus or other invader, produce a variety of substances, collectively known as lymphokines, designed to repel the foreigner; interferon is a familiar one. Some also act as "helpers" in the B-cells' operations—marshaling phagocytes, for example—while others act as "suppressors," restraining inappropriate B-cell activity.

A second, similar virus, now known as HTLV-2 (the first is now called HTLV-1), was later identified. And still later, the most notorious of the retrovirus family was recognized: First labeled HTLV-3, it is now called HIV, for human immunodeficiency virus, and it causes the acquired immunodeficiency syndrome—AIDS. (Actually, that should be plural as well, since a second, less widespread virus, named HIV-2, has also been identified.)

Now there are hints that a retrovirus may be involved in lupus, and in a related disorder as well.

In chapter 2, I talked about Raynaud's phenomenon (or syndrome, or disease), which may occur alone or as an accompaniment to lupus. Another such sometimes-stand-alone, sometimes-not condition is Sjögren's syndrome, which involves dysfunction of various moisture-producing glands, predominently those that produce saliva and tears, causing extreme dryness in the affected area(s). About one in twenty lupus patients suffer from this syndrome as well.

In early 1992, researchers at the University of Texas in San Antonio announced that they had found antibodies to proteins that are components of HIV in approximately 30 percent of a group of Sjögren's syndrome patients and in a similar proportion of a group of lupus patients. There was no indication that they had antibodies to HIV itself, only to certain proteins; as the investigators explained, the findings suggested that they had developed antibodies to an *HIV-related* virus—that is, another retrovirus—not that they had been exposed to the virus that causes AIDS. Researchers at the Pasteur Institute in Paris have also reported finding such antibodies in the majority of a small group of patients—five out of eight—with active lupus; all eight had lymphopenia, abnormally low levels of lymphocytes.

But this intriguing discovery presents still another puzzlement: If this retrovirus sets the self-destructive lupus process in motion, it behaves very differently from the AIDS virus—in a contrary manner, in fact. In AIDS, the immune system apparently falters because the primary cells depleted by HIV are the "helper" T-cells, key players in the body's defense system. The result is that people with AIDS succumb to infections, and other conditions such as certain cancers, normally fended off successfully; more than two-thirds of the deaths in AIDS are caused by lung infections.

In lupus, quite the opposite is true: There is a marked deficiency of "suppressor" T-cells—with an eight- to tenfold *increase* in the proliferation of antibody-producing B-cells. It appears, in fact, that among those antibodies are some directed specifically against "young" T-cells that are in the process of developing into suppressors. Thus, these two related retroviruses must do something very different to the lymphocytes they infect—one killing off "helper" cells, the other depleting the population of "suppressor" cells (assuming the existence of this second virus).

Two sidelights on the retroviral question, both reported at a 1991 National Institutes of Health (NIH) conference on lupus:

1. Some HIV-infected people have developed lupus, though probably no more than would be expected among the population in general. But at least three children born with HIV infection (which is transmissible in pregnancy) have developed lupus; this was unexpected and unusual.

2. Individuals who already have lupus and become infected with HIV often experience remission of their lupus, perhaps because of decreased "helper" T-cell activity leading to diminished B-cell production of antibodies.

Whatever the infectious agent—if there *is* an infectious agent involved—some researchers have postulated that the self-destructive activity evident in lupus may involve something beyond the ordinary antigenic effect of the usual bacterium or virus, a sort of "super-antigen." Only one such super-antigen has been shown to be definitely associated with human disease: The ubiquitous bacterium *Staphylococcus aureus* ("staph"), under certain circumstances, produces a powerful toxin; that toxin causes the condition called toxic shock syndrome. Investigators are seeking such a reaction, both in lymphocytes from patients with autoimmune diseases and in strains of mice that serve as experimental models for these diseases.

I personally believe that when the primary cause of lupus is found—and it *will* be found, eventually—it will turn out to be a virus, whether a retrovirus or some other type, that behaves in an unusual manner (or is *permitted* to behave in an unusual manner in some individuals, perhaps those with particular genetic characteristics). As some have suggested, a super-antigen may be involved. But I am more inclined to another theory: that of "slow virus" behavior, denoting a virus that causes an initial illness, then lingers in the body and causes a distinctly different illness at a later date. We do know of viruses that behave in this manner. Most of the handful of conditions traced to such a mechanism are limited geographically and are not seen in the U.S. or Europe, but there are exceptions.

One example is Dawson's encephalitis, or subacute sclerosing panencephalitis, usually referred to as SSPE. It causes insidious, gradual deterioration of the brain, with neuromuscular, sensory, and mental disintegration. In the past, its victims were typically between the ages of five and twenty, most of them boys (the reason for the gender imbalance is not known). There is no treatment, and death is inevitable.

Early research in SSPE had revealed strange structures or particles in brain tissue; they were described as "myxovirus-like." Later, specific antibodies were investigated, and markedly elevated levels of antibody against the measles virus were found in SSPE patients. Finally, in 1970, the measles virus itself was isolated from the brains of SSPE victims. The conclusion was that SSPE is due to reactivation of the virus—which has remained lurking in the body, somehow eluding antibodies primed to destroy it—in someone who has had measles. With routine immunization of children against measles (a vaccine was introduced in 1963), the incidence of SSPE has declined markedly.

What makes a virus behave in this manner? Clearly, some agent or factor must "awaken" the virus—and permit it to survive during the period between the initial illness and the reactivation. Aside from the sex imbalance, SSPE in this country has always occurred more often in the Southeast than in other areas. And one study found that in a significant number of SSPE cases, there had been contact with a dog suffering from canine distemper (which is also caused by an RNA virus).

Certainly some special conditions must exist to permit SSPE to occur. Before there was a vaccine, measles was a very common childhood illness—but SSPE was extremely *un*common. Progressive rubella panencephalitis, a similar condition which can develop about a decade after initial infection with that virus, is even rarer. (A rubella vaccine was introduced in 1969. It was later combined with measles and mumps vaccine, and a single injection of MMR vaccine is now given routinely at the age of fifteen months.)

Another condition in which parallels with lupus (as well as SSPE) can be drawn is multiple sclerosis (MS). Like lupus, MS is an autoimmune disorder, but in MS, the immune system attacks only one sort of tissue: a substance called myelin, which sheathes nerves; as the sheath disintegrates, it is replaced by scar tissue. Like lupus, MS typically strikes in the twenties or thirties (there is no particular sex preference). As in lupus, there seem to be familial connections; a relapse-and-remission pattern is common; and some association with HLA markers— notably, DR2 and DR4—has been observed. Like lupus, MS is chronic and may have no particular effect on life expectancy (although it is often extremely debilitating).

Like SSPE and unlike lupus, MS is more likely to appear in

certain geographical areas than in others. Worldwide, it is most prevalent in cool temperate zones, between 40° and 60° latitude (both north and south); it is some forty times more common in Minnesota, for instance, than in Mexico City.

Interestingly, some studies have shown that when people migrate from one area to another, the "risk" migrates as well. And age seems to be a factor. Among those moving from a "high-risk" to a "low-risk" area, or vice versa, after the age of fifteen, the prevalence of MS reflects that in their native climate. Such observations are consistent with MS's being related to a viral or other agent more widespread in temperate than tropical areas and typically acquired in childhood.

As in lupus, various studies in MS patients have unearthed viral connections. Many researchers, over the years, have reported unusually high levels of antibodies to the measles virus, and some have found myxovirus-like or paramyxovirus-like fragments. More recently, investigators have detected the presence of retroviral particles that appeared to be HTLV-1 or something very much like it.

Doubtless the most familiar family of viruses that are capable of this sort of thing is the herpesvirus clan, whose members persist in various types of body tissues, seemingly impervious to any immune-system sentinels. They may emerge again and again to cause recurrent episodes of the same condition, like the herpes simplex viruses, which linger in skin and mucous membrane and cause cold and canker sores and genital lesions. Or they may trigger a completely different problem on subsequent appearances; the varicella-zoster virus—which causes chickenpox, retreats to nerve tissue, and causes shingles on reemergence—is the prime example.

One other class of infectious agents must be mentioned, for the sake of completeness, although it has not (yet) been explored extensively in connection with lupus. Mycoplasmas are distinct microorganisms, neither bacteria nor viruses. The first one isolated, around the turn of the century, causes sickness in cattle, and most mycoplasmas are associated with nonhuman ills, including arthritis in swine, chickens, and turkeys. Only a few species have been linked to human disorders, including pneumonia, some cases of infertility, and recurrent miscarriage. (Some mycoplasmas target the respiratory tract, others the genitourinary tract.) A small urinalysis study reported in the spring of 1992 by Harvard researchers found mycoplasma infection in 63 percent of a series of lupus patients and in only 4.5 percent of control subjects.

There is, of course, the possibility that the development of lupus—as well as other autoimmune disorders—requires a combination of two or more infectious agents simultaneously attacking a genetically susceptible individual and setting off an unstoppable immune-system reaction. Or perhaps the virus ("slow" virus or other) or other attacker is aided and abetted by some other factor in the individual's life (or lifestyle). Which brings us to a final question:

## Other Environmental Agents?

It's frequently been observed that certain things can worsen lupus—sunlight, for instance. About a third of lupus patients are photosensitive (sensitive to ultraviolet light); sunlight can set off a flare-up of quiescent disease, not just in the skin but elsewhere in the body as well. Sunlight alone surely doesn't *cause* lupus—but might it play a role in conjunction with another factor, such as a virus?

Some medications, including such common antibiotics as tetracycline, can induce and/or enhance photosensitivity. As I noted at the beginning of this chapter, some drugs, and some other substances as well, can actually induce a lupus-like syndrome that remits with removal of the inducer. Could such drugs or other chemical substances play a role—again, in combination with genetic, viral, or other factors—in the usual kind of lupus as well? No one knows.

Another phenomenon suggesting some role for environmental factors is the coincidental occurrence of autoimmune disorders in pet owners and their pets. While most diseases affect either animals or humans but not both, there are exceptions, including such viral infections as the infamous swine flu and equine encephalitis, and fungal infections like ringworm (the latter is easily caught by children from puppies and kittens).

And dogs, as the nation discovered in mid-1991, can have lupus. In May of that year, President George Bush received a diagnosis of Graves' disease, an autoimmune disorder of the thyroid gland. His wife, Barbara, has the same condition, diagnosed at the beginning of 1990. And in the summer of that year, the Bushes' springer spaniel, Millie, was found to have lupus.*

This situation is, to put it mildly, extremely unusual. According to newspaper reports, the Bushes' physicians called the coincidence "bizarre," and a variety of experts were said to have estimated that the odds of a husband and wife both developing Graves' disease were from one in one hundred thousand to one in three million—not to mention the odds of such a couple's also having a dog afflicted with an autoimmune disease.

---

*Canine lupus, first described in 1965, is now based on the same diagnostic criteria as lupus in humans. The most prominent symptom is polyarthritis—involving many joints—which afflicts nine of ten animals with the disease. About 60 percent have skin or mucous membrane lesions, and almost two-thirds have kidney involvement.

A common cause, perhaps? A virus? Some other infectious organism? Table scraps shared with Millie? Furniture, fixtures, or some other factor in the family wing of the White House?

And then there's Teeny, now five years old. She belongs to Jan, whose lupus was diagnosed only a year and a half ago—but who, you may recall, describes symptoms over several years. Teeny is a charming and altogether lovable, albeit not overly swift, tabby. As Jan recalls, "I got these two cats at the same time—they were both about five weeks old—and it was clear that Teeny had some congenital problems. I found out after a while that the blank stare was because her pupils don't dilate properly. She's always been, well, sort of floppy; she's never learned to jump like other cats. At the age of five years, her idea of a challenge is still chasing her tail. I have one cat and one kitten who'll never grow up."

Teeny became physically ill at the age of six months: "The diagnosis was autoimmune hemolytic anemia. The vet said, 'This is very rare in cats, and it never comes back.' It came back a year later, and it has come back again and again. The bouts of it have become more frequent, especially in the last two years, and I can tell when it's coming on: She gets tired easily. She plays less. She gets mad when her hips are touched, and she won't let me squeeze her paws to trim her claws. She drinks much more water than usual. She's now taking corticosteroids; I just hope she'll be all right."

"Is this just a coincidence," Jan wonders, "or did she catch a virus from me? Or is there something in the environment we share—something to which we're susceptible, but my husband and my other cat aren't?"

There is some disagreement on whether Teeny's illness or any such illness in cats can properly be termed lupus, although all her signs and symptoms—anemia, fatigue, apparent joint and muscle discomfort, extra fluid consumption—can be found in human lupus. But whatever its name, it's evidently an autoimmune problem.

Has anyone undertaken a scientific study of this sort of phenomenon? Yes, on a small scale. A group of immunologists in England did so and reported the outcome in 1992 in the British medical journal *The Lancet.* Fifty lupus patients were randomly selected from the researchers' hospital register and asked about dog ownership; only pets that lived in the house with their owners were included in the study. All the dogs were apparently well. Blood tests were done and the results compared with tests on a group of certified healthy animals which served as controls, as well as tests on a group of dogs with a definite diagnosis, or at least marked evidence, of autoimmune disease.

As expected, significantly more anti-DNA antibodies were found in the dogs known to be ill than in the control animals— but the average for the lupus patients' dogs was even higher. Additionally, all the blood samples were subjected to serum protein electrophoresis testing, which reveals unusual levels of antibody-containing immunoglobulins; abnormal patterns were found in 33 percent of the patients' dogs and in 44 percent of the autoimmune-disease group but in none of the controls.

The study was a small one, and the results do not prove anything—about the cause(s) of autoimmune disease in people, the cause(s) of autoimmune disease in dogs, or what they may have in common. The researchers cautiously concluded, however, that the findings "lend support" to the idea that "common environmental factors or transmissible agents" may play a role—and that further research along these lines would be worthwhile.

# CHAPTER

# 4

# Doctor and Patient: A Delicate Partnership

Medicine is classed as a science, but it is far from an exact one. In some areas, there is little or no disagreement among its practitioners: All physicians would agree that smoking cigarettes is harmful to your health, that a bacterial infection is best treated with an antibiotic (they may not necessarily agree on *which* antibiotic), and that it is wise to have physical checkups at intervals (they may not agree on *what* intervals).

But in many ways, medicine is more art than science, and physicians' experience, coupled with their philosophies and attitudes, may well affect how they choose to assess facts and apply scientific knowledge. In this chapter, I want to talk about such considerations as they might affect the treatment of lupus—and more specifically, the lupus patient. That treatment depends very much on having a doctor on whom you can rely for both crisis management and, as important, continuing support.

## Finding a Physician

Your physician is the person to whom you entrust your health. That means you should have full confidence in the physician's professional abilities *and* feel comfortable with his or her attitudes and approaches to you and your illness. This applies in any patient-doctor relationship; it applies especially to lupus—a chronic, unpredictable disorder demanding a high degree of patient-physician teamwork.

If you have unexplained symptoms and you think you may have lupus, or your general internist or family physician suspects you may have lupus, you should be referred to (or you should seek) a board-certified rheumatologist. A rheumatologist is a physician who has chosen to specialize in internal medicine and to subspecialize further in rheumatology, the branch of medicine dealing with lupus, rheumatoid arthritis, and related disorders.

Any licensed physician may develop an interest in particular parts of the body, classes of patients, or kinds of ailments, and may then describe himself or herself as, for example, an orthopedist, pediatrician, or allergist. Such a physician may even possess above-average skills. "Board-certified" means that the physician not only has an interest in a specialized area but has passed examinations attesting to his or her expertise. A board-certified physician, also referred to as a diplomate of the particular certifying board (in this case the American Board of Internal Medicine), will display—or can produce, upon request—a document to that effect.

It's best if the physician deals with nothing *but* rheumatology; while practice may not always make perfect, it does lead to greater depth of knowledge and acquaintance with the spectrum of illness within that area.

How do you locate a qualified person if you haven't been referred by your primary-care physician? Two very good ways: (1) Contact the nearest major medical school or teaching hospital (hospital affiliated with a medical school); direct your inquiry to the department of medicine (in medical schools, that means internal medicine) and ask for several recommendations. (2) Put the same question to your local chapter of the Lupus Foundation or the Arthritis Foundation; either should be familiar with the leading specialists in your area.

Aside from board certification, what should you look for in this physician with whom you are likely to have a long-term relationship?

Probably most important, look for what the *physician* looks for. What I mean by that is this: You are a unique individual. A good physician will not view you as Lupus Case (or Possible Lupus Case) Number 337 but as a human being experiencing health problems. The physician should want to know everything about you that might have a bearing on those problems, everything that might define them and lead to solutions.

You should, of course, receive a thorough physical examination. You should be asked for samples of blood and urine for analysis (other diagnostic tests, as well as X rays, may also be needed). And you should be questioned about:

- the symptoms and complaints that brought you to this physician, with attention to timing (when did they start? do they come and go? are they connected with particular times, places, or activities?);

- *any other* physical problems you've recently experienced;

- whether or not you smoke;

61

- recent weight gain or loss;
- any medications you take regularly or frequently, both prescription and nonprescription;
- your general lifestyle, including the work you do;
- your recent travel, especially outside the country;
- past major illnesses and operations;
- any allergies or other chronic conditions;
- if you are a woman, your menstrual and reproductive history.

Then, you'll want to ask some questions of your own, especially relating to availability. Is someone on call when your own physician is on vacation, or attending a conference, or teaching medical-school classes? Who is that person? (Sometimes a group or associate practice, with patients' records readily available to each physician, is a good idea.) If you should need to be hospitalized for any reason, where would that be? (Depending on the community, physicians may admit patients to one, two, or more hospitals.)

The physician may volunteer something of his or her approach to treatment; if not, feel free to ask.

And you may want to consider other questions of a practical nature—convenience of transportation, for example, if you're choosing among physicians located at various distances from your home. Does the doctor have a "telephone hour" when patients can call with routine, non-urgent questions?

Your own instinctive reactions will—and should—play a part, too. Are you more at ease with a female physician, or with a male physician? Do you feel better with an older (presumably more experienced) doctor, or with a younger (presumably more up-to-date) one? Neither of these presumptions is necessarily true, but they may affect your own comfort level.

Physicians, like other people, have personalities. Some are terse, others verbose. Some are brusque and matter-of-fact; others go out of their way to encourage and reassure. Some explain in detail; others talk in generalities. Patients, like other people, have preferences. Some like a take-charge, just-leave-it-to-me doctor; others would rather be privy to all the nitty-gritty details. Some grudge time spent in the doctor's office; others see those visits as valuable opportunities to explore concerns. Does this physician's style and personality mesh with yours? You need to decide for yourself whether or not you think you'll be compatible.

Should you be forced to choose between a physician of unquestioned professional excellence who scores low in congeniality, and a charming sort with questionable professional credentials, you'll be wise to opt for the former.

If you've been referred to a rheumatologist by your regular doctor, the rheumatologist may either undertake your treatment or report back with a confirmation of the diagnosis and recommendations for therapy; it depends on what seems best for you. Typically, especially if you don't have other major medical problems, your lupus will be managed by the subspecialist, who'll keep your regular physician informed.

## A Plan of Action—Or Inaction

There is a cardinal principle of the practice of medicine which is learned by every future physician in medical school, faithfully observed by most, but unfortunately occasionally forgotten by a few: *Primum non nocere.* This Latin phrase means, "First of all, do no harm." In lupus, in which severely disruptive drugs must sometimes be used to control or dispel severely destructive or debilitating disease processes, this prime directive translates into, "Treat the patient, not the lab tests—and don't *over*treat."

Laboratory tests do play an initially important part in establishing the existence of lupus, basically confirming a diagnosis the experienced rheumatologist has made on the basis of examining and talking with the patient. Mainly, lab tests rule out other conditions—malignancies, endocrine-gland diseases, specific organ dysfunctions—requiring very different treatment. They also establish baseline values for later comparison.

Beyond those roles, lab tests are not necessarily terrific predictors of treatment needs.

The aim is to keep the patient as healthy as possible—which means, essentially, two things: controlling and relieving symptoms that interfere with the quality of life; and preventing and coping with critically threatening complications, such as kidney disease. Lab-test results are not always indicative of the patient's status in either sense.

Indeed, there is often apparent contradiction between lab tests and how the patient is actually feeling and functioning. In many cases, patients with test values traditionally viewed as alarming—high erythrocyte sedimentation rate (ESR), low levels of serum complement, and high levels of anti-dsDNA antibodies—remain perfectly well and free of complications with little or no treatment. Because lupus *does* present the threat of serious complications, both patient and physician must, of course, remain alert for worrisome signs or symptoms—but that needn't, and shouldn't, mean taking unnecessary drugs.

As I pointed out earlier, very few lupus patients ever need to be hospitalized. Nor do a great many lupus patients need to be on the massive drug regimens on which they are, too often, placed. Some doctors seem to be unaware that a person who has lupus need not necessarily take any medication. Therapy should be keyed to symptoms—and even so, need not involve drugs.

Fatigue, for example, is often a prominent symptom. If it becomes totally debilitating, and nothing else works, medication may be needed. Frequently, however, another "prescription"—a combination of diet modification, rest, and a certain amount of specific exercise—will be wonderfully effective. Lupus is a condition in which disease activity, what lupus patients and their physicians call a "flare," is provoked by unknown factors including substances the patient may encounter in the environment. In such a condition, it makes little sense to introduce other, potentially trouble-making substances unless they're clearly needed.

Of course, medications *are* frequently needed, to deal with discomfort or with disease that threatens vital functions. When medications are prescribed (see the next two chapters), your physician should indicate clearly how and when they are to be taken, for how long they should be taken, and any precautions you should observe—including interactions with foods and with other drugs. If there's anything you don't understand, ask.

## The Ongoing Relationship

You'll recall Connie, who'd had some joint discomfort as a teenager and been told she had rheumatoid arthritis; had suffered pregnancy complications a decade later; and finally, a few years after that, told her gynecologist of fatigue and mouth sores and decided, on his advice, to see a rheumatologist.

"He did tests," says Connie, "and he told me a test for being predisposed to blood clots was negative. Beyond that, he was very uncommunicative; you had to drag information out of him. Not only that—you always waited two hours to see him, and then he rushed you out of the office. I went for about a year, trying different anti-inflammatories, and I finally decided to change doctors. I found another rheumatologist, and I had my records transferred from my old doctor to the new one."

Connie's first visit to her new physician was an eye-opener: "My new rheumatologist said, 'Ah, you have lupus.' I said, 'No, I have rheumatoid arthritis.' He said, 'No, see, here in your records. You have lupus.' The first doctor hadn't even told me my diagnosis!"

Your continuing relationship with your doctor can be crucial to your health, in a number of ways. Erosion of the relationship can cause you to question your physician's advice, rightly or wrongly—and to disregard that advice, wisely or unwisely. It can cause you to deceive your doctor, intentionally or inadvertently. It can play havoc with communication between you. If nothing else, it can upset you emotionally, and that is not something a lupus patient, or *any* patient, needs.

Your goal and your physician's goal are the same: to maintain an optimum state of health for you. The achievement of that goal requires, at the very least, mutual respect and honesty.

Respect, on the physician's part, means recognition of your independent status as an individual, not only as a patient. Such recognition is evidenced by concern for your identity as a human being, including your occupational, parental, and/or other roles. It is evidenced by concern for your time: While emergencies do occur, and some schedule disruptions are beyond the physician's control, patients should not routinely be kept waiting to see the doctor for inordinate lengths of time, in either reception room or examining room.

A respectful attitude also accords you dignified treatment: Your conversation in the doctor's office does not take place only with you unclothed on an examining table; there is subsequent discussion across a desk. And unless the physician is markedly your senior, you are not addressed by your first name unless and until permission is asked. (First-name usage should always be mutual.)

Respect is a responsibility of the patient as well—again, in both a professional and personal sense.

Your physician wants what you want, your health and well-being, and is applying his or her knowledge and expertise to that end. Grant that effort the respect it deserves by following your doctor's carefully thought-out advice and instructions. (Failure to follow that advice, of course, "cheats" only the patient.) Offer feedback as well: Your doctor needs to know if the treatment plan is working or not, if medication has caused side effects, if new symptoms have appeared; only you can furnish that information.

Respect your physician's working schedule by keeping appointments and advising the doctor's office promptly if something prevents you from doing so. Recognize that your physician has another life—family, friends, recreational pursuits—as well, and cannot be available to patients at all times; when you must consult with the substitute your doctor has selected, give the stand-in the same respect you would your own physician.

Honesty between patient and physician is absolutely vital and really part of their mutual respect. Obviously, Connie's first rheumatologist was grossly dishonest in failing to inform her of her diagnosis.

Beyond that basic expectation, how much information is provided may depend, to a degree, on your own wishes. Some patients are fascinated by medical minutiae; others prefer to be told only what they need to know and not be burdened by complex scientific details. In either case, you deserve to be dealt with frankly and openly. Your questions should be answered to your satisfaction. If you express confusion or confess ignorance, you should receive explanations, not evasions.

By the same token, you must be honest with your doctor. That means answering questions—about your symptoms and feelings, about your habits and lifestyle, about your compliance with your doctor's advice and recommendations—fully and forthrightly. In fact, it's in your own self-interest to do so, since in great part your input provides the primary "data base" for your doctor's plan of therapy, especially in the case of lupus.

Even with the best efforts on the part of both patient and physician, however, some such partnerships just don't work out. Never feel that you must remain with a particular physician. The first certifying examinations in rheumatology were given only in the 1970s; even a decade ago, it might have been difficult to find many "boarded" physicians from whom to choose. Now, many more are available. If you're not happy with the first rheumatologist you see (or you eventually become unhappy), seek another—or another referral from your primary-care physician. Don't worry about hurting the deserted doctor's feelings; he or she will get over it.

Two important reminders:

1. Don't forget that there are other specialists everyone must see regularly: an ophthalmologist for eye examinations; if you're a woman, your gynecologist for Pap tests (to detect incipient cervical cancer) and a clinic or other facility for mammography (special X rays to detect early breast cancer); your dentist for checkups on your oral health.

2. Always make sure every doctor you see knows what the others have prescribed. Various medications may interact dangerously with others, rendering them either more or less potent; can have side effects that could be confused with symptoms of illness; and can distort the results of laboratory tests.

## Beyond Doctoring: The Take-Charge Patient

Your physician can examine you, order and interpret laboratory tests, diagnose your disease, prescribe medications, and refer you to other professional providers of health care. But your doctor can't make other decisions for you—big decisions like whether or when you'll pursue conception or practice contraception; day-to-day decisions on what to eat, when to sleep, how to order your waking hours. You may well find that some reconsideration—of priorities, of goals, of relationships—is in order.

Probably if one pervasive frustration were to be cited, a frustration for physicians and patients alike, it's the unpredictability of lupus. Some patients develop an uncanny sense of incipient flare:

"Flares are almost always related to travel," reports Connie, "and they're definitely brought on by stress and letting myself get overtired. I can pretty much predict them."

"I can tell when a flare is coming," says Nancy, "because I get depressed. Well, actually, I don't really know if the flare causes the depression, or I get depressed about something and that brings on the flare."

Most, though, are taken by surprise.

"Absolutely the worst part is the unpredictability," declares Lisa. "You never know what's going to happen. There is no rhyme or reason to this disease. You can't make plans."

Jan is deeply resentful: "I'm angry. I know there are a lot of things you can't control in life, but I always thought I could control myself. To be out of that control—to be unable to know for sure the day before whether I'll be able to do what I plan to do tomorrow—is *terrible*."

In my own observation, flares often follow marked stress. Precipitating stresses can be either physical or emotional, or a combination of the two. Many are completely unpredictable—an acute infection or injury, a sudden death in the family, the loss of a job, the breakup of a long-term relationship. But others can be anticipated; I have seen flares when patients have simply demanded too much of themselves and, for example, scheduled too many work and social commitments (what used to be called "burning the candle at both ends") or overloaded their academic schedules the first year of college.

From experience in treating hundreds of lupus patients, and from past medical history of an individual patient, I can make an educated guess about the effects—and side effects—of a prescribed medication. But I can't know with absolute certainty that the drug will perform as we hope. I can't promise a flare-free future; I wish I could, but I can't. Neither can *your* doctor.

Nor can your physician be with you through the ups and downs of your life, which will inevitably interact with your lupus. Only you can relate the many facets of your life to one another and take positive steps to control these interactions—at least, to a far greater degree than anyone else.

In the chapters ahead, I'll spell out a great many details of medications and other therapies, both the up and the down sides, because it's important that the patient know as much as possible. In the end, all treatment decisions are really yours; your doctor can only recommend, provide relevant information, and advise.

I also want to offer some insights—beyond the basics of diagnoses and medical interventions—that can help you in making day-to-day judgments and taking charge of your life. Those insights range from understanding the risks of pregnancy through awareness of chemical troublemakers and possibilities for effective self-therapy. Lupus, as you know, is a very individual disease, and what works very well for one person may not work for another. But I hope, and believe, that you'll find *something* of value for *you* and *your* situation.

Talking about "attitude" has become something of a cliché, but the comments that follow may be well worth heeding.

Nancy admits that there are times when she feels angry about having lupus and sorry for herself, "But most of the time, I don't. I think of myself as a healthy person who happens to have lupus. I *have* lupus; *I* am not lupus."

"I had an interesting experience at my rheumatologist's office a couple of weeks ago," says Elizabeth, who has been experiencing the ravages of what was probably lupus for more than two decades, although her diagnosis didn't come until the mid-1980s. "I came into his office, and a young couple were sitting there. I started to back out, but he invited me in to talk with them, while he left the room. She had just been diagnosed and was very depressed. She said, 'People say, you don't *look* sick.' I said, 'Wouldn't it be worse to look the way you feel? Isn't it better to look well?' Why visit your discomfort on your friends? You have to ignore some of what you feel physically, because it won't change. The whole thing is attitude. In dealing with a chronic disease, you need to accept it and simply do your best to cope."

As Eileen puts it: "Sometimes I'm frustrated. There are days when I feel sorry for myself, but I *allow* myself to feel that way. I may even lie down and cry for a while, and that's okay. But I don't get really angry, because I've seen what anger can do. My mother has had several illnesses; she is very angry, and that just compounds all her problems. Anger can be so destructive. You need to give yourself permission to feel some fury when you first find out the diagnosis—but you deal with illness the way you deal with life. I confront things, learn as much as I can about them, and try to find out what I can do."

And, she adds, she takes a certain comfort in the good times: "When I'm feeling great, I really appreciate it, and I can enjoy life a lot more. I have a mild enough case to realize that I'm very lucky—so far, anyway—not to have major organ involvement, and to be symptom free so much of the time. Of course, I'd love for it to go into complete remission, forever. But I still know, on bad days, that it's only a matter of days or weeks. I can hang in there. Listen, everybody's going to get something. I know what I've got, and I just figure out how to deal with it the best I can."

I hope to help you do just that.

# 5

# Drugs Used for Lupus

As I pointed out in the last chapter, using unneeded drugs never makes good medical sense, and it's especially unwise in lupus. Nevertheless, medications are sometimes needed.

Drug treatment of lupus has progressed through three general stages over the last few decades. Roughly until the post–World War II period, the approach was what might kindly be called trial and error—or, more bluntly, hit or miss. Little had been established as to potential risks or potential benefits. Among the many let's-try-it-and-see-if-it-works substances employed were gold (some forms of which *are* effective in rheumatoid arthritis), bismuth, liver extracts, and an array of vitamins.

Subsequently, a number of specific drugs were found to be truly helpful in various manifestations of lupus. Unfortunately, their benefits were recognized before their range of hazards was fully realized. They came to be overused, in both dosage and duration of treatment, with the result that patients were sometimes made sicker by their medicine than by the malady the medicine was meant to allay. And since some medications may give rise to symptoms not unlike those of lupus itself, the temptation to heap drug upon drug was probably understandable in some cases.

Happily, there has been a reversal. The trend is now toward conservative treatment—meaning a stance in favor of administering or prescribing medications only when they are clearly needed, and then only in the quantities necessary. Not that all lupus patients, in all circumstances, are always so treated. I commented in chapter 4 that lab tests don't necessarily reflect a patient's actual state of health. Nevertheless, some of those who treat lupus seem to focus on the lab tests, "treating" the tests rather than treating the patient.

As I've noted, other-than-normal values on blood tests may even turn up in people who don't have lupus at all. When such test results occur in relatives of patients, they may suggest interesting possibilities regarding familial factors in the cause of lupus. When they occur in persons who share a patient's home or workplace, they may set off intriguing speculation about environmental influences. But no one has ever suggested that those people should receive any treatment.

Patients themselves *may*, however, need drug therapy. Let's take a look at the medications that, when used appropriately, are indeed valuable in the treatment of lupus.

Most prominent among those medications are those known as corticosteroids. They will be prescribed for almost every lupus patient at some time, whether on a short- or long-term basis, and both their benefits and risks are many and complex. I've devoted the entire next chapter to them.

Several other kinds of medications have also been found frequently helpful for treating various facets and manifestations of lupus.

## The Antimalarials

"Fatigue has been a problem," says Connie. "Our vacation last summer was really awful. We went to a resort in New York State, and we'd planned to do all kinds of things, but we ended up just staying in the lodge the whole time. Then I went on Plaquenil. Since it kicked in, I've been doing much better."

Nancy has had rashes, including the renowned butterfly rash, and she found Plaquenil solved that problem. "My rheumatologist," she adds, "told me it would take about six weeks to start working—and it did, almost to the day."

The antimalarials—drugs originally used in the treatment of malaria—were the first of the specific agents found helpful for lupus that are still employed; they've been in widespread use since the late 1940s. Quinine—the classic antimalarial—had been tried experimentally in lupus as early as the 1890s, and some related drugs enjoyed favorable reports a generation later, in the 1920s, when it was found that they seemed to be effective in clearing up cutaneous lesions associated with lupus.

Now, a number of quinine derivatives, known collectively as chloroquines, are used—notably, chloroquine (Aralen), hydroxychloroquine (Plaquenil), and quinacrine (Atabrine). They're helpful not only for the skin but for joint manifestations and fatigue as well. Some studies have also suggested—but not yet proved—that continuing therapy, particularly with hydroxychloroquine, may make flares of disease activity less frequent or milder. They are *not* effective for, and shouldn't be relied on for, the treatment of serious kidney, heart, nervous-system, or blood complications. And patients should be aware that six to eight weeks or more may go by before their benefits are evident.

Elizabeth took chloroquine for a while; now, she must have an eye examination every three months.

Lisa took chloroquine until very recently: "I went to the eye doctor, and he said he thought he saw changes. I saw a second eye specialist, and he determined that there is chloroquine retinopathy—even though I have 20/20 vision, and I'm not aware of any problems when I'm reading, or out walking, or driving. They find this through something called field of vision tests. The medication has now been stopped. My doctor kept telling me to go for checkups; I should have gone earlier."

Like all drugs, the antimalarials may have side effects, including scaly rashes and stomach upsets; the latter, according to one limited study, are the most common complaint but still affect only a minority of patients, perhaps one in five, at least with hydroxychloroquine, the most widely prescribed. Even hydroxychloroquine, generally considered the least risky antimalarial, has not been proved safe for a developing fetus, and so an antimalarial will generally be discontinued several months in advance of a contemplated pregnancy. With these drugs, though, the most worrisome impact is on the eyes.

A number of effects involve the cornea, the transparent membrane covering the pupil at the front of the eyeball. Deposition of the drug in this area may result in blurred vision when the medication is started and "halo" radiation around lights later on. This has not been seen with quinacrine—but with quinacrine, corneal edema (swelling) can occur, due to fluid accumulation. Corneal anesthesia, in which the ability to feel pain is deadened, may occur with any of these drugs; that could prove dangerous in case of accidental injury or overexposure to sunlight. All of these effects disappear once the medication has been discontinued.

More serious is an irreversible condition involving the retina, the area at the back of the eyeball where images are focused and from which they are relayed to the brain by the optic nerve. It is called macular retinopathy; it involves pigment deposits and is apparently related to both drug dosage and degree of individual photosensitivity.

The risk of this toxic reaction seems to be higher with chloroquine than with the other members of the family, but patients taking *any* of these drugs should take three precautions:

1. Always wear sunglasses—preferably, not only in bright sunlight but also when the sun is not shining and, if possible, indoors as well as out. Be sure they are of high quality and bar ultraviolet light.

2. Avoid direct exposure to unshielded fluorescent or halogen lights.

3. Have your eyes thoroughly examined by an ophthalmologist—a physician specializing in the eyes—before you start taking the drug (to establish a baseline) and at regular intervals thereafter, so that the drug can be promptly stopped if there is any sign of retinal injury. This examination is vital, since the retinal deterioration is symptomless. Discuss the frequency of these checkups with your rheumatologist; the question is related to the specific drug and dosage, and recommendations may range from every three months to annually. These drugs have a long half-life (they remain in the body for some time), so continued eye exams may be indicated for a number of months after cessation of the medication, as Elizabeth's physician has advised.

By and large, most rheumatologists feel that the safest of the antimalarials, and the least likely to cause critical irreversible side effects, is probably hydroxychloroquine—and the drug has recently been shown to have a couple of incidental "side effects" that are highly beneficial. Reports at two major medical conferences in 1992 suggested that hydroxychloroquine may lower levels of the lipids (cholesterol and kin) that may clog arteries and promote coronary heart disease; prednisone, a corticosteroid (see the next chapter), can raise those levels, and adding hydroxychloroquine may be protective. It may also diminish the risk of dangerous clot formation in those with a tendency to that risk; it is, in fact, used in Europe to prevent such complications following surgery.

## The NSAIDs

There is a large group of medications almost always used in rheumatoid arthritis and used by most of us at one time or another to relieve many types of discomfort. They are classed as nonsteroidal anti-inflammatory drugs—NSAIDs (pronounced "*en*-sades") for short—which simply means that they act against inflammation but are not steroids (which are discussed in the next chapter).

Some NSAIDs, such as aspirin and ibuprofen (Advil, Motrin, Nuprin), are available over the drugstore counter without prescription; many others are not. (You may wonder why I haven't mentioned acetaminophen, sold under such brand names as Datril, Liquiprin, Tempra, and Tylenol. While it is at least as widely used as aspirin to relieve minor aches and pains and reduce fever, it does not have any significant anti-inflammatory action, hence is not useful in conditions, including arthritis, where inflammation is the major problem.)

Aspirin and other drugs related to it are known as salicylates ("aspirin" was once a trade name for what is chemically acetylsalicylic acid), and they are sometimes helpful in lupus when the chief complaint is joint pain. The dosages, however, are higher than those the labels recommend for the usual purposes, and they are often taken on a regular schedule rather than simply in response to discomfort.

Be warned that the salicylates, despite their widespread availability and use, are *not* innocuous drugs, especially in lupus. Take them in higher than over-the-counter label doses only on your physician's advice, and follow your doctor's recommendations for quantities and timing.

The salicylates are used much less in lupus than in rheumatoid arthritis. Only one of the patients we've been following in this book, Connie, currently takes one of them—salsalate, also known as salicylsalicylic acid (Disalcid).

A vast array of nonsalicylate NSAIDs is available by prescription, far too many to list here. It sometimes seems, thumbing through the medical journals, that a new variation or formulation is introduced almost monthly. There is some validity to the seemingly infinite numbers, however, since some seem to work better than others for particular patients—so that if one doesn't seem to be effective, or ceases to be effective, the physician has many others from which to choose.

Unacceptable side effects can also dictate discontinuing a particular drug. With the NSAIDs, a common problem is gastrointestinal irritation, particularly with the salicylates; with long-term use of the drugs, ulcers may develop. Aspirin is available in buffered and other forms to diminish such reactions, and many of the prescription products introduced in recent years have been formulated specifically to avoid the possibility of such irritation. If you are taking an NSAID, your doctor may suggest antacids; or a protective anti-ulcer medication such as cimetidine (Tagamet) or ranitidine (Zantac) may be prescribed to prevent problems.

Another not-uncommon side effect, particularly with salicy-lates, may be ringing in the ears (medically called tinnitus), although those who experience it are in a distinct minority. Headache and fatigue are among other occasional reactions to NSAIDS, as are rashes, bronchial spasm, or other manifesta-tions of allergy. (People allergic to aspirin may have similar reactions to some other NSAIDs.)

Some of the prescription products may have even more serious adverse effects, among them impairment of kidney function, exacerbation of hypertension, anemia, liver disease, and blood-count abnormalities. Three of the NSAIDs—ibuprofen (Motrin et al., plus nonprescription-dosage brands), sulindac (Clinoril), and tolmetin (Tolectin)—have been known to trigger aseptic (nonbacterial) meningitis; I have also seen one case of meningitis associated with (although not necessar-ily caused by) a fourth such drug, naproxen (Naprosyn). Although it can occur in anyone taking these drugs, lupus patients seem to be more susceptible to the reaction. Headache and fever are the chief initial symptoms.

Any unexpected symptoms, however mild, or worsening of prior symptoms that may occur while you are taking any drug should be promptly reported to your physician.

## Immunosuppressants

The corticosteroids (see the next chapter) might be referred to as immunosuppressants, since they act, in part, by quelling im-mune-system activity. But the kinds of drugs generally meant by this term are agents used to prevent the rejection phenomenon in organ transplants. They also interfere with the proliferation of quickly multiplying cells and are used to treat some malignancies. The rationale for their possible use in lupus: they may reduce the ranks of B-cells that are producing antibodies.

Prominent among those that have been tried in lupus are azathioprine (Imuran) and cyclophosphamide (Cytoxan). The word "tried" must be emphasized. These agents are not considered standard therapy for lupus and, when they *are* used, they are reserved for critical complications. They have never been under consideration for treating the less serious manifestations of lupus, such as rashes, arthritis, or fatigue.

There have been many clinical trials conducted over the years; still, firm conclusions have not been reached. A study of patients with serious kidney inflammation, conducted by the National Institutes of Health (NIH) and reported in 1991, concluded that while azathioprine wasn't of significant help, cyclophosphamide in combination with prednisone did seem to be effective in preserving kidney function.

Other investigators have generally concurred in that assessment, and most recent clinical trials have focused on cyclophosphamide, either in combination or in comparison with corticosteroids, testing various short- and long-term courses of therapy and various dosages. Another NIH study, reported at the 1992 international conference on lupus, compared pulse therapy—relatively high doses given by intravenous injection at specific intervals (of days, weeks, or months)—using the two types of drugs. The researchers found long-term pulse cyclophosphamide (administration frequency changed over the trial duration from daily to quarterly) superior to similar therapy with a corticosteroid in a group of lupus patients with severe kidney inflammation. Other researchers at the same conference reported both similar and conflicting findings, but different regimens were followed in the various trials. All of these trials used the pulse technique.

In late 1992, an NIH team reported results of a small study (only ten patients) employing oral cyclophosphamide to treat active kidney inflammation. The therapy seemed to be effective and relatively well tolerated, and the researchers concluded that it might be a reasonable alternative to corticosteroids.

The powerful immunosuppressants do have side effects, ranging from slight to severe. Since their prime action is suppression of the immune system, they lower resistance to infection. Serious effects are more likely with intravenous administration, but infections termed "minor" did occur in the oral-cyclophosphamide study mentioned above, with one patient developing shingles, another cellulitis, and a third a urinary-tract infection.

Among other documented consequences: gastrointestinal disturbances, hair loss, hepatitis, bone-marrow suppression with resultant anemia, oral candida infection ("thrush"), sterility, hemorrhagic cystitis (bladder inflammation with bleeding) and, uncommonly, certain cancers.

## Remedies for Raynaud's

Earlier, I mentioned a condition that can occur alone and also affects a significant proportion of people with lupus—Raynaud's phenomenon, the condition that first sent Nancy to consult a rheumatologist.

Raynaud's affects circulation to the fingers (less commonly, the toes; rarely, the earlobes or tip of the nose) so that they become numb and discolored, as if frostbitten—not only in cold weather but under other stressful conditions as well, which may vary with the individual. The cause is vasospasm, spasmodic constriction of arterioles (the smallest arteries) resulting in cut-off of peripheral circulation. It's exacerbated by smoking, so quitting is the first therapeutic "prescription." In the past, not much could be done beyond that and hand-warming devices.

A class of drugs called calcium channel blockers, introduced relatively recently for the treatment of coronary heart disease, has been found beneficial in Raynaud's as well. One in particular, nifedipine (Procardia), has proved effective in various trials for 65 to 90 percent of patients suffering from this condition.

The drug is available in both oral (i.e., to be swallowed) and sublingual (under-the-tongue) forms. Patients who have found regular oral administration either ineffective or intolerable due to side effects (some people experience very low blood pressure, headaches, dizziness, or ankle swelling) often find that the sublingual form, used shortly before exposure to cold, can prevent an attack and is free of side effects.

## Some Precautions . . .

Before I go on to discuss the major class of drugs prescribed for lupus, I want to say something about medications generally.

Lupus patients may often be on a relatively complex medication regimen. Fatigue and emotional ups and downs, as many patients have found, can sometimes play havoc with efficiency and straight thinking. It's a very good idea to write down all medication dosages, schedules, and other particulars, or to have your physician do so, so that no mistakes are made.

Be sure to ask, too, exactly *when* and *how* the medication should be taken—i.e., time of day and relation to meals. Some medications should be taken with food, or a certain amount of time before or after eating, or on an empty stomach; some should not be taken with certain types of foods; some pills should not be taken with certain liquids. This kind of information does not usually appear on your pharmacy's label.

If you know you're among those lupus patients who are photosensitive, which means that sunlight can trigger rashes or other symptoms, let any physician or dentist prescribing for you know about that right away. Some drugs can intensify photosensitivity, and the doctor who is forewarned will select an alternative medication.

Similarly, let doctors know ahead of time about allergic or other reactions (rashes, stomach upsets, and so forth) you've had in the past, to *any* medications. Depending on the seriousness of the reaction, this may mean that you should not take a particular drug, that a class of drugs should be avoided, or simply that certain protective measures (against stomach irritation, for example) need to be taken.

Remember to keep your physician completely informed— about any unexpected symptoms (which may mean side effects, lupus activity, or something else entirely), about whether a new medication plan is working or not, about drugs prescribed by any other doctor. And let other doctors you may consult know exactly what drugs you're taking for lupus.

## . . . and a Safety Note

All of the medications employed in the treatment of lupus—in fact, most medications that may be taken for *most* ills—can be extremely hazardous, and even fatal, to infants or toddlers who may ingest them accidentally. Small children have peculiar senses of taste and smell, are not particularly discriminating, and may gobble down lethal doses of even foul-tasting substances. "Childproof" containers (which sometimes aren't, for a child with better-than-average dexterity) may not make sense for a patient with hand and finger joint involvement.

If there are small children in your home, or small children might visit your home, keep your medications completely out of possible reach, preferably under lock and key. This applies to all medications, prescription and nonprescription.

# CHAPTER

# 6

# The Main Medicines: Corticosteroids

As I've said, corticosteroids will be prescribed for almost every lupus patient at one time or another. Like most medications, they have advantages and disadvantages—but with these drugs, the "ups" and the "downs" are perhaps more extreme. They have more than once been termed "double-edged swords."

Don't confuse this group of drugs—often referred to simply as "steroids" by physicians and patients alike—with another, widely publicized group of substances called by the same familiar name.

The term *steroid* is actually a catchall designation for an array of organic compounds, based upon details of their chemical structure at the molecular level. Substances classed as steroids include, among others, cholesterol, bile acids, some vitamins, and many hormones; among the latter are testosterone and other androgens, as well as estrogens and some of the hormones produced by the adrenal glands.

You may have read or heard about the "steroids" used illicitly by athletes and some teenagers. Their full name is *anabolic-androgenic steroids.* They are synthetic testosterone derivatives, and they are taken for their skeletal-muscle-building (anabolic) effects; they are also masculinizing (androgenic) and, as used by those young men (and a few women), extremely hazardous to health.

The drugs discussed in this chapter, the corticosteroids, while extremely potent, do not pose the perils of those testosterone derivatives. The corticosteroids, however, do have their own benefits and risks.

## The Benefits

Eileen, you'll recall, found she had lupus only after a routine blood test revealed abnormalities and a battery of other tests confirmed the diagnosis. The only prior clues to something amiss had been her presumed false-positive test for syphilis and the acutely painful bout of arthritis she'd suffered as a result of a reaction to sulfa drugs.

In fact, she'd never really experienced lupus symptoms, although the blood tests said she *had* lupus. Six years later, that changed: "I was under a great deal of stress. By this time, I'd managed to set up a little antiques-and-collectibles shop, and I was working eighty-hour weeks, and my mother became seriously ill. Suddenly, I was really sick. My symptoms were mainly fatigue, low-grade fever, and painful joints, with swelling in my hands and feet. Would you believe I was so busy it was three months before I saw the doctor?"

For the next year and a half, Eileen took a variety of NSAIDs, chiefly one called sulindac, although, she says, "It controlled my symptoms only slightly. I still had a lot of pain, and terrible fatigue. My rheumatologist kept saying, 'You should go on prednisone.' But I didn't want to, because I'd heard about the side effects, mainly weight gain."

Curiously, an incident not directly related to lupus changed Eileen's mind: "It was August. I was still trying to be active, I had my business under better control, and I'd decided to get away on a two-week vacation; I was planning a bike trip in France with a friend in September. One day, I was sitting outside, and a caterpillar fell onto my leg. That night, I woke up with flaming welts. I called my dermatologist, who prescribed prednisone. I called my rheumatologist, who said it was okay. The welts cleared up in one day. I finished the prednisone prescription, and I immediately had excruciating joint pain. I was supposed to be packing for my trip that night. I called my rheumatologist the next morning and said, 'Put me on pred-nisone. I'm not missing this trip.' He started me on ten milli-grams. By that night, I could move. The next day, I was *much* better. I continued to improve, and I did go on the bike trip."

The trip went well, with minimal pain, and on her return, Eileen and her doctor gradually reduced her daily dose of the drug to three or four milligrams, with no problems. "But I was worried," she says. "I wanted to do some more traveling—I love to travel—but what would I do if I were halfway around the world and symptoms came on? Then, I got a case of stomach flu, and it kicked up everything. My doctor had told me that infection, as well as stress, can kick off a flare. He was right. I was a basket case. We increased the dosage to seven milligrams."

As far as Eileen was concerned, that proved something of a miracle. "It was like a light went on," she declares. "All of a sudden, I felt I was in control. I've continued on prednisone—

I haven't had any remission since then—generally on five milligrams; if I have bad symptoms, I go to seven. I'm no longer in fear of travel; I just take along both five- and one-milligram pills, so I'm prepared. I know every case of lupus is different, and I figured seven was my magic number. But my doctor says it works for other patients, too, because that's the level the body manufactures normally."

"And," she adds, "I haven't had any side effects. Not only haven't I gained weight, which I had while I was taking the other drugs. I've managed to lose a few pounds through not being so stressed, eating right, and getting exercise."

Prednisone is one of the corticosteroids, also sometimes called glucocorticoids and often simply steroids for short; occasionally, in older writings, they are referred to collectively as "cortisone." This family of agents resembling cortisol, a hormone produced by the cortex of the adrenal glands, are without doubt the drugs that have been found most useful in lupus. There are a number of versions, including prednisone (the most widely used), prednisolone, methylprednisolone (Medrol), dexamethasone, triamcinolone, cortisone, hydrocortisone, and many more. As with the NSAIDs, one may be more helpful than another for a particular patient.

These drugs play a part in therapy for a number of ills in addition to autoimmune disease, including respiratory distress in premature babies, certain cancers, asthma, migraine headaches, and severe allergic reactions. (Of course they are also used as replacement therapy in failure of the adrenals to produce the natural substance, just as thyroid hormone or insulin is given to patients who cannot produce the needed levels of those substances.) In lupus and other autoimmune conditions, they have the effect of controlling symptoms, primarily by anti-inflammatory action and possibly by inhibiting the production of antibodies. Generally, they are prescribed in low dosage, to be taken on a regular basis (maintenance dosage); taken in somewhat higher doses, for limited periods of time, to cope with flares of disease activity; and administered in huge amounts, often by injection, to deal with major crises such as deteriorating kidney function.

Eileen's comment on "normal" levels, by the way, is correct: A dose of six or seven milligrams does approximate the body's usual secretion. But many patients require higher dosages to meet their needs. Elizabeth, like Eileen, regularly takes five milligrams a day, while Lisa reports that, "When I started getting pleurisy frequently, my rheumatologist started me on prednisone. I now take a maintenance dose of between ten and fifteen milligrams, more if I get pleurisy."

## The Drawbacks

Unfortunately, the corticosteroids can have a number of serious side effects, typically related to long-term administration and/or high dosages, so that under most circumstances, dosages will be kept as low as is feasible, and the drug will be gradually tapered off entirely if possible.

Among those possible effects are: weight gain; increased susceptibility to infection and/or masking of symptoms of infection; slowed healing of injuries; easy bruising; unusual hair growth; cataracts; precipitation or worsening of diabetes mellitus; amenorrhea (absence of menstruation); coronary artery disease (possibly related to increased lipid—cholesterol, et al.—levels); aggravation of peptic ulcer (sometimes considered a contraindication for these drugs); facial swelling ("moonface"); elevated blood pressure and lipid levels; sleep problems; mood swings or mental disturbances;* reactivation of latent tuberculosis (persons with positive skin tests for TB should receive prophylactic anti-TB drugs if they must take corticosteroids); and the precipitation of glaucoma-like pressure buildup within the eyeball.

The foregoing reactions may vary with the individual. Some other effects, effects that occur consistently, need to be noted.

One is the fact that the steroids suppress production by the pituitary gland of the hormone ACTH (adrenocorticotrophic hormone), the normal function of which is stimulation of cortisol production by the adrenals. This happens because the medication results in an "ACTH unneeded" message to the pituitary. Taking the drug in the morning minimizes the effect, because ACTH production is highest between 4 A.M. and 8 A.M.; corticosteroids taken in the evening can suppress it totally.

Nancy's first encounter with prednisone followed a potentially alarming event: "About a year and a half ago, I had some kidney involvement. I noticed that my urine was a funny color, like weak tea, and I called my rheumatologist in a panic. I was sent to a radiologist for a sonogram, and I also had a lot of blood tests and twenty-four-hour urine tests. They apparently showed a lot of hematuria and proteinuria."

Eventually, a renal biopsy—a sampling of kidney tissue—confirmed that she was suffering from nephritis, kidney inflammation: "I had pulse therapy, with prednisone, which is three days of 1000 milligrams per day, intravenously. I had it

---

*If you have previously had psychiatric problems—or there is any family history of psychiatric problems—it's imperative that you mention this to your physician *before* you take one of these medications. The steroids that have been most often associated with adverse mental effects are hydrocortisone, dexamethasone, and prednisone.

again a month later and again three months after that, and that seemed to resolve it. I go every three months for urine tests, and I now take prednisone orally; I started with twenty milligrams on alternate days, and I now take fifteen milligrams on alternate days."

Jan, who is on a multiple-drug regimen to control her multiple symptoms (it includes Plaquenil and indomethacin, an NSAID; see the previous chapter), has a similar steroid schedule: "I take Medrol [methylprednisolone] on alternate days, in varying doses, depending on how I'm doing. Right now, I'm taking twenty-eight milligrams; it's been as low as twelve and as high as forty milligrams. I've had weight gain because of the Medrol," she adds, "directly because of it, plus it gives you a tremendous appetite. My weight keeps going up and down."

With the shorter-acting steroids—prominently, prednisone and methylprednisolone—alternate-day therapy, taking the medication every other day rather than daily, is believed helpful in decreasing side effects due to suppression of normal hormone production. This is not true for some other drugs in the steroid family, such as dexamethasone and triamcinolone, which persist in the body for several days.

After withdrawal of corticosteroid therapy of long duration (meaning several weeks or more), there is an extended period of hormonal imbalance, with a deficiency of the natural adrenal hormone. Cortisol's normal function is helping the body withstand sudden, massive stress. During corticosteroid therapy and for at least a year thereafter, serious injury or surgery calls for prompt steroid supplementation.

Women who take corticosteroids should be aware that these drugs are apt to encourage osteoporosis, skeletal weakening due to loss of bone substance, resulting in a heightened risk of fractures. See chapter 8 for more about this important concern.

Because of the increased susceptibility to infection, anyone taking steroids should be sure to avail themselves of appropriate immunizations. For adults, that means flu vaccine (plus pneumonia vaccine if your physician thinks it advisable). For children, that means the routine schedule of childhood immunization, plus flu vaccine and special precautions or treatment on being exposed to, or contracting, chickenpox (at this writing, no chickenpox vaccine has been approved for general use); see chapter 13.

A comment on the question of weight gain, which Jan reported as a problem and Eileen reported as a fear which didn't materialize: Corticosteroids can cause some fluid retention, but the resulting gain is very minimal. Significant weight gain is mostly a matter of increased appetite and, as Eileen and others have demonstrated, that's possible—though not necessarily easy—to overcome, with effort and determination.

None of the systemic effects I've mentioned apply to the corticosteroid creams and ointments that can be purchased over the counter, without prescription, and are used to treat skin conditions.

CHAPTER

# 7

# Other Problems, Other Treatments

In chapters 5 and 6, I reviewed the drugs that have been used to control and contain lupus and its common manifestations. When those medications prove inadequate, or if additional symptoms or complications develop—due to lupus *or*, sometimes, to the drugs themselves—other therapies may be indicated. Some are tested and have been relied upon for years; others are just now emerging on medicine's technological frontier.

## Alternatives for Anemia and ITP

One example of a situation in which other treatments will be explored is that of anemia that proves refractory to drug treatment.

"Anemia" is a broad term simply meaning a deficiency of red blood cells, not specifying the cause of that shortage. It can be caused by blood loss, for example, as in injury or surgery, or internal bleeding from a peptic ulcer (or stomach lining irritated by aspirin or other drugs). Prolonged, uncontrolled inflammation can also cause anemia, by disrupting the body's handling of iron, which is used in the production of new red cells.

Another sort of anemia is termed *hemolytic*, a word coined from two Greek ones that translate as "blood destruction." In the normal course of events, our bodies constantly produce new cells and discard old ones. An individual red blood cell lives for about four months and is ultimately sequestered and destroyed by the spleen; in hemolytic anemia, red cells are disposed of prematurely, after as short a time as hours to weeks. Many things can trigger hemolytic anemia, including toxins, bacteria, and drugs.

Anemia is not unusual in lupus, affecting about 50 percent of patients to one degree or another. A common kind is autoimmune hemolytic anemia, in which antibodies produced by the body itself attack its own red cells. Prednisone is usually effective, but not always. When it is not, splenectomy, surgical removal of the spleen, may be necessary. Blood transfusion may also be needed when anemia is severe.

A condition called immune thrombocytopenia (ITP) may also arise in lupus (it can also occur independently); the causative mechanism is similar to that of autoimmune hemolytic anemia. Thrombocytopenia is a deficiency of thrombocytes, also called platelets, the blood cells that are necessary for normal clotting. Symptoms may include nosebleeds, gums that bleed easily, or petechiae—small, spontaneous "bruises" that signal tiny hemorrhages in the skin. Repeated episodes of ITP may well have caused the bleeding problems Elizabeth experienced (page 27). Again, prednisone may remedy this condition, but in some cases, splenectomy is needed.

Removal of the spleen, which may be necessary in some other conditions as well, generally causes no ill effects, and its normal tasks are assumed by the liver and lymph nodes. The one exception is that after splenectomy, an individual is more susceptible to pneumococcal infection* as well as salmonella infection; pneumococcal vaccination is therefore recommended for those who have had splenectomies. The levels of protective (antibacterial) antibody should be checked after vaccination and at intervals thereafter, since a decline over time has been reported in some lupus patients.

## Two Musculoskeletal Complications

As if the painful arthritis that afflicts so many people with lupus weren't enough, another joint problem, osteonecrosis, may arise in up to 20 percent of those who take corticosteroids, typically after treatment over a long period of time. (Less commonly, it has been known to occur in lupus in the absence of steroid therapy.) Statistically, it seems to be more prevalent among lupus patients who also experience Raynaud's phenomenon. One recent study, by rheumatologists at the University of Connecticut, has also linked its occurrence with the presence of anti-cardiolipin (ACL) antibody, but in another study seeking associations with various antibodies, Johns Hopkins University researchers found no such connection. (This antibody, which has major significance for pregnancy, is discussed in chapter 9.)

---

*The bacterium *Streptococcus pneumoniae*, also called pneumococcus, is one cause of pneumonia, which may also result from infection by other bacteria, viruses, and other organisms.

Osteonecrosis is also known by other names—aseptic necrosis of bone, ischemic necrosis of bone, avascular necrosis of bone—and is a deterioration of the bone due to diminished blood supply. Theoretically, any joint can be affected, but weight-bearing joints are most frequently involved. By far the most common is the hip, and the affected site is the head of the femur, the thighbone. (Second- and third-ranking joints: the knee and shoulder.)

Pain during use of the joint is the initial symptom; sometimes, the pain may at first not be felt in the joint itself but is referred to a nearby area—in the case of a hip, the groin, the buttock, or even the knee. Later, there is pain while the joint is at rest as well. Some time may go by, from months to as long as five years, until the damage is detectable on X rays, but other techniques, such as bone scans and magnetic resonance imaging (MRI), may confirm the condition earlier and should be used if there are symptoms but X rays show no departures from normal.

If osteonecrosis is not treated, it will progress and eventually cause serious dysfunction. Conservative treatment—watching, waiting, and resting the joint—has generally not worked well. The sole exception has been the shoulder joint, where a program of restricted motion plus special exercises has been reported to be successful in about half the cases.

With other joints, the first-choice treatment is a surgical procedure called core decompression. In this operation, a small core of tissue is extracted from within the ischemic (blood-deprived) area of the bone, serving two purposes. It relieves pressure on the microcirculation in the problem area and stimulates formation of new capillaries and healthy bone; and the extracted tissue is analyzed to confirm the diagnosis. The technique, which has been in use only since the mid-1970s, is often successful in staving off progress of the necrosis and postponing the necessity for major surgery.

"It's hard to tell," says Lisa, "whether some of my problems over the past few years are from the lupus or from the prednisone. One thing I've had is avascular necrosis of the hip. I had a core decompression about five years ago; so far, it's working, although I'll probably end up needing a replacement eventually. And I've severed tendons like they were spaghetti, including the tendons in both of my thumbs—one of them twice—and a patellar tendon. It happens with very simple things; one of the thumbs, I was just picking up a bag of oranges. I've had seven surgeries in the last seven years."

Once osteonecrosis has progressed far enough to be evident on X ray, core decompression is no longer an option. Lisa mentioned "replacement"; she was referring to total joint replacement. That surgery may become necessary eventually, especially in the case of a constantly weight-bearing joint such as the hip or knee; it may be the only possibility if diagnosis has come too late for decompression.

Great strides have been made in joint surgery, technically termed arthroplasty, in recent years. The first operations to replace the ball-and-socket joint of the hip were performed in the early 1960s, and this was the first joint-replacement surgery to be pronounced an unqualified success. The complicated hinge joint of the knee posed greater technical challenges, and the surgery was still considered experimental in the 1970s. Those challenges have now been met successfully. By 1990, an estimated 120,000 hip replacements, and an equal or greater number of knee replacements, were being performed in the United States each year.

Another type of therapy for avascular necrosis, at this writing strictly experimental, is under investigation. It involves the application of an electromagnetic field to the affected area over a period of time and can be carried out at home. Whether or not this technique, which has been found helpful in promoting the healing of fractures, will be equally useful for osteonecrosis remains to be seen.

Lisa also mentioned "severed" tendons. The term more often used is tendon *rupture,* and it's quite common. Here, too, the basic cause is avascular necrosis and, again, it can occur with or without steroid therapy. The tendon becomes frayed and can rupture easily—as Lisa observes, with little or no physical strain involved. Probably the most common site is the little finger, the pinkie, which abruptly drops; a patient, suddenly unable to lift the finger, may fear she has suffered a minor stroke. Repair of a ruptured tendon requires surgery.

## Return of a Virus

"I thought it was hives," says Eileen. "It's always on my rear end. You can feel it starting, tingling; within two hours, there are these eruptions the size of a dime and up. I never had a handle on what caused it. Then, I happened to be at my gynecologist's near the end of one episode, and I mentioned it. He took one look and said, 'That's shingles.' He prescribed acyclovir, which cleared it up within three days."

It's happened to Lisa, too: "I've had shingles three times in the last three years. I never knew, before this, that you could have it more than once. I guess that's because of the prednisone."

Steroids, as I've mentioned, do disrupt the immune system, and recurrent shingles is indeed not uncommon among lupus patients—assuming they have had chickenpox, which is caused by the same virus, one of the singularly unpleasant family of herpesviruses. Most familiar of these viruses is the herpes simplex virus (HSV), which comes in two forms; type 1 commonly causes cold sores and canker sores, type 2 genital lesions.

Chickenpox and shingles are the popular names for varicella and herpes zoster, and the virus responsible for both is known as the varicella-zoster virus, or VZV. There is, at this writing, no vaccine yet available for general use, although one will probably be approved soon.

An initial infection with VZV causes chickenpox. The virus, like other herpesviruses, then remains in the body—emerging, when circumstances are congenial, to trigger an episode of shingles, a painful skin eruption that typically occurs somewhere on the trunk, in a pattern literally following the nerves where the virus lurks between appearances. Most people will suffer shingles only once—although theoretically, they *could* experience repeated episodes; lupus patients often do.

Acyclovir (Zovirax), mentioned by Eileen, is one of the few antiviral drugs available thus far, and it's generally considered the most effective—specifically, against HSV and VZV. Acyclovir is usually given orally for shingles. (The drug is also available in intravenous and topical forms.) At this writing, it has not been proved safe in pregnancy, although there have been no reports of serious adverse effects.

Lupus patients experiencing an episode of shingles should avoid close contact with pregnant women who have never had chickenpox, since chickenpox—i.e., initial VZV infection—poses possible risks of complications to both mother and child.

## Recourses for Renal Dysfunction

One of the most critical threats in lupus is renal (kidney) dysfunction. About half of all lupus patients have some renal involvement, which may or may not ever progress to a critical, or life-threatening, stage; hypertension (high blood pressure) appears to raise the risk of kidney problems. Terms used for inflammatory changes in the kidney include *nephrosis, nephritis, glomerulonephritis,* and *nephrotic syndrome.* (The *-osis* suffix suggests degenerative changes, while *-itis* denotes inflammation. "Renal" simply means "relating to the kidneys"; it derives from the Latin word for kidney, *renis.* To describe disease involving the kidneys, medicine has opted to use terms derived from the Greek word for kidney, *nephros.* )

Continuing deposit of antigen-antibody complexes in the glomeruli, the minuscule tufts that comprise the kidney's filtering apparatus, can eventually cause total impairment of function in that vital area. The result is that waste materials, instead of being flushed from the body, remain in the circulation. Untreated, uremia—the medical term for this bloodstream pollution—leads inevitably to increasing mental and physical deterioration and, ultimately, death.

A lupus patient's kidney function is therefore constantly monitored. A key clue is assessment of the creatinine clearance rate. Creatine is a substance, produced by the liver, that furnishes energy for voluntary-muscle contraction. Enzyme conversion in the muscle in turn produces a waste product called creatinine, which is normally excreted in the urine. A high blood-creatinine level indicates a low clearance rate, suggesting serious kidney dysfunction.

Another assessment that may be performed is a test for BUN, which stands for blood urea nitrogen; the test determines the portion of blood-borne nitrogen derived from urea, a metabolic end-product that is another usual component of urine. Again, high levels may hint of kidney dysfunction. This test is less definitive, however, since elevated BUN may occur in conditions other than renal disease, and may also be caused by certain drugs (which may actually raise the levels, *or* may affect the accuracy of testing).

A third diagnostic procedure may be kidney biopsy, removal of a small amount of kidney tissue for microscopic examination. Physicians differ on the advisability and necessity of kidney biopsy, and the subject is somewhat controversial.

Twenty or twenty-five years ago, kidney biopsies were performed routinely, even when nothing in the urine suggested any trouble. Some still feel that the procedure is vital, in order to determine the exact nature and stage of possible kidney deterioration. Others believe it isn't necessary to subject the patient to this procedure, except under very special conditions, such as a sudden rather than gradual decline in kidney function; that could signal renal vein thrombosis (clot formation), a critical condition requiring prompt intervention in the form of anticoagulants or even surgery.

My own feeling on the matter of kidney biopsy is that it can be of great value in some situations but doesn't need to be performed in every instance of suspected kidney dysfunction. Certainly if urinalysis turns up nothing unusual, there is no indication for biopsy. But if urinalysis shows that renal function is deteriorating, biopsy can be of great value, since the findings can help in selecting appropriate therapy.

It should not, however, be undertaken lightly. It is a surgical procedure and, like all surgical procedures, it is not risk free. When I feel kidney biopsy is warranted, I advise the patient of that risk. I also explain what testing has shown, what a biopsy may reveal, and—depending on the findings—the various treatment options.

I might, for example, suspect from urine and blood testing a particular sort of kidney condition called diffuse proliferative nephritis, which I know from experience responds well to treatment with cyclophosphamide. I would share that suspicion with the patient and discuss with her the therapy I will recommend if the biopsy confirms my suspicion—both its benefits and its substantial hazards. If the patient says she would not wish to risk that therapy, then there is no point in performing the biopsy.

When kidney impairment has become potentially life threatening, and medications are ineffective—a level of impairment referred to medically as "end-stage renal disease"—there are two possible recourses.

One is hemodialysis, periodically filtering the patient's blood through a mechanical device outside the body (an "external kidney") to remove waste materials. The procedure has been literally a lifesaver for many patients. Overall disease activity and need for medication are likely to decrease when patients are receiving dialysis and, importantly, survival rates increase markedly.

Five-year survival rates among patients who have had dialysis have been approximately 85 percent; in one major study reported in 1990, the ten-year survival rate for a group of patients on dialysis was 75 percent, comparing favorably with the 83 to 93 percent figures cited in the introduction for lupus patients as a whole. In a minority of patients on dialysis—30 to 40 percent—the deterioration is reversible; they may recover renal function and be able to discontinue dialysis.

The second alternative is kidney transplant, and patients who have received dialysis for a while have sometimes subsequently opted for transplant. First performed successfully in 1954 between identical twins, the surgery has now become routine, due largely to three factors: the development of ways to keep a kidney viable over many hours and many miles, careful histocompatibility matching between donors and recipients (see page 40 for more on that subject), and improved drugs to dampen rejection reactions.

By 1977, kidney transplants had already become so common that the International Human Renal Transplant Registry decided to stop bothering to keep track of them; its final report put the world total then at close to 25,000. Now, approximately 10,000 are performed annually in the United States alone.

In the mid-1970s, the Registry estimated the five-year graft (transplanted organ) survival rates at 78 percent for sibling kidneys, almost 75 percent for parent-to-child grafts, and over 50 percent for kidneys from unrelated donors. The figures for lupus patients have not differed from those for others receiving transplants, and recurrence of lupus nephritis in the transplanted kidneys has been rare. (Failure of the *graft* to survive does not mean the *patient* will not survive. When a transplanted kidney fails or is rejected by the recipient's immune system, it can be replaced.)

Since then, histocompatibility (HLA) typing and matching has steadily become more sophisticated, and the graft survival figures reflect that improvement. In 1987, a collaborative study involving all transplant centers in the United States was begun under the auspices of the United Network for Organ Sharing (UNOS); its aim was to compare graft survival of HLA-matched transplants with others, not thus matched. (Matching was done at the A, B, and DR sites; again, see p. 40 for an explanation.) It was recognized that HLA typing meant that the best match, when a donor organ became available, might be a recipient as far away as the opposite side of the country; thus, more time would elapse before the transplant could take place.

Results for over 1300 transplants were reported in late 1992, and HLA matching proved to make a significant difference. The rate of graft survival at one year among the 1004 patients receiving a first kidney transplant was 88 percent for those that were HLA matched, versus 79 percent in recipients of mismatched organs. Based on these figures, the investigators estimated graft survival would be 17.3 years in the first group, only 7.8 years in the second—less than half the projection for the matched cases.

The impact of HLA matching apparently lessens when a patient has already had a transplant. Among patients receiving a kidney transplant for the second time, the one-year graft survival figures were 80 percent for matches, 74 percent for non-matches. And among those who received a third or fourth graft, matching didn't seem to confer any particular advantage in terms of graft survival at all.

Shipping the kidneys to distant recipients, with a longer out-of-body interval, didn't negate the benefits of HLA matching, the investigators observed. Survival of matched grafts transplanted after thirty-six hours still exceeded that of mismatches transplanted within twenty-four hours. Also, graft survival appeared higher when the kidney donors were under the age of fifty.

With kidney transplant a truly lifesaving possibility for those with lupus nephritis—it is also considerably less costly than dialysis—it is unfortunate that so many patients are unable to benefit from it. By late 1991, some 19,000 people in the United States were waiting for renal transplantation. The problem is a shortage of donor kidneys. (The problem exists, too, for other transplantable organs, such as hearts and livers.)

Nearly 80 percent of kidneys donated for transplant come from people who have recently died in accidents or of other causes not affecting the health of their kidneys. The Uniform Anatomical Gift Act has made it possible for people to carry a card, with legally binding language recognized in all states, authorizing that their organs be donated in case of death. But fewer than 15 percent of our citizens carry donor cards; in the absence of such directives, distressed families must make organ-donation decisions at an already difficult time. All in all, it's estimated that only 15 to 20 percent of suitable organs from recently deceased people actually become available for transplantation.

Postscript: The multicenter UNOS study has demonstrated without question that HLA matching has significant impact on graft survival—and that national allocation of available kidneys makes sense, rather than limiting options to what may be available within twenty-four hours locally. That raises a question: Should the length of a patient's wait for a new kidney, or the likely length of graft survival as determined by HLA typing, be the prime factor in deciding who receives available organs? Perhaps, as some have suggested, a "point system" taking both factors (as well as other medical considerations) into account would be desirable.

Although the closest HLA match is almost invariably found in one's own blood relatives, taking a kidney or other organ from a living individual represents a major hazard to that person, because of both the surgery and loss of the organ. Therefore a matched cadaver organ is preferable.

CHAPTER

# 8

# Osteoporosis: Detection and Prevention

As I mentioned in chapter 6, among the many unfortunate side effects of corticosteroids, which are part of many lupus patients' regimens at one time or another, is a tendency to promote osteoporosis ("porous bones"), skeletal weakening due to loss of bone substance. This condition generally afflicts women after menopause (see discussion of that topic in chapter 11, page 181)—but steroids increase the risk at any age.

Osteoporotic bone is prone to easy fracture, even in the absence of outright trauma. One collaborative study at Johns Hopkins University and the University of Maryland, reported at the 1992 meeting of the American College of Rheumatology, found that 6 percent of the lupus patients at the two medical centers had sustained at least one fracture since their lupus was diagnosed; one in four of them had suffered multiple fractures.

The most common fracture sites were the hip/femur (thigh-bone), vertebrae (spine), and ribs, in that order. Those who had had fractures were somewhat older than those who did not (about half had been through menopause), were on higher steroid dosages, and were also more likely to have experienced osteonecrosis (see the last chapter, page 95).

There are a number of factors, in addition to taking steroids, that increase the risk. Statistics tell us that osteoporosis occurs more frequently among women who: are smokers; are of Scandinavian descent (Caucasian women in general, as well as Asian women, are more susceptible than those of other races); are thin and small-boned; experienced any periods of amenorrhea (absence of menstruation) in their teens or twenties (not uncommon in athletes, as well as in young women with eating disorders); had low calcium intake when they were young; or have had close relatives with osteoporosis.

Osteoporosis is typically symptomless until a fracture occurs. The spinal fractures are typically not spinal-cord-threatening injuries; they are painful compression fractures of the vertebrae, usually in the upper back, which curve the spine into the sadly familiar "dowager's hump." (This disfigurement, medically termed dorsal kyphosis, is not only unsightly but hazardous to health: The postural aberration can contribute to accidental falls and, because the chest cavity is compressed, it can also contribute to pulmonary problems.)

If osteoporosis is occurring, it needs to be detected promptly. X rays alone are not totally reliable for this purpose; a more sophisticated technique called dual-photon bone densitometry is better. If you are approaching or have passed the menopause, or are taking steroids (whatever your age), scanning should be performed regularly, at whatever intervals your physician recommends.[*]

# How It Happens

Most people assume that, once adult stature is attained, bone is more or less static. In fact, human bones continue to grow in strength and density until the mid-thirties, when peak bone mass is achieved.

Like all other tissues in the body, bone is constantly broken down (resorbed) and replaced; in bone, the process is known as remodeling. Bone consists of a protein framework, called the osteoid matrix, in which calcium—the chief constituent of bone (as well as teeth)—is deposited. Certain cells, called osteoclasts, do the breaking down of old bone, while other cells, called osteoblasts, are responsible for building new bone. Various other substances, including calcitriol (the active form of vitamin D, also known as 1,25-dihydroxycholecalciferol), the thyroid hormone calcitonin (sometimes called thyrocalcitonin), and parathyroid hormone, play important roles at various points in this cycle.

The rate of remodeling varies among individuals, and it also varies with the two types of bone. These differ in structure. Trabecular, or cancellous, bone, which has a lattice-like structure, is characteristic of the spine; it remodels somewhat faster than cortical, or compact, bone, which is found primarily in the long bones of the arms and legs (overall, about 80 percent of the

---

[*]It must be noted that scans to measure bone density are often not covered by health-care insurance. Many insurance companies, unfortunately, decline to cover preventive and diagnostic procedures that could conceivably help to avoid complex and costly remedial procedures in the future.

human skeleton consists of cortical bone).

After the mid-thirties, the rate of resorption begins to exceed the rate of rebuilding. The result: decreased bone mass and density. Effects are slight at that point, and the decrease is very gradual, approximately 0.5 percent a year. It accelerates, however, at the time of the menopause in women and about the mid-seventies in both sexes (although women are affected by this spurt more, as well).

Bone also functions as a repository for calcium, which is not only a bone-building material. Calcium is vital to a number of other processes, including neural transmission and blood clotting. It also plays a crucial role in muscle contraction (that includes the heart as well as other muscles, both voluntary and involuntary).

A relatively constant reserve of calcium, about 1 percent of the body's total, is maintained in the bloodstream to meet these additional needs. Whenever that circulating supply drops below the demand, it's brought back up to the required level by drawing upon the bones' stores. Depletion of this store of calcium without replacement triggers the insidious process of osteoporosis.

The drop in available estrogen at menopause is associated with a speed-up of bone resorption, and the reason smokers raise their risk of osteoporosis is that smoking results in abnormally low levels of circulating estrogens. One theory of the significance of estrogen holds that its depletion somehow upsets the balance in the numbers of osteoclasts and osteoblasts, resulting in an oversupply of the former and a shortage of the latter. The body's ability to absorb calcium apparently slackens after menopause as well.

The major direct cause of osteoporosis is a shortage of calcium. While steroids may have a direct effect on bone cells, stimulating osteoclast activity and inhibiting osteoblasts, their major impact is on the calcium supply, since they reduce intestinal calcium absorption. (Heavy alcohol consumption has the same effect.) In high doses or long-term administration, they are also believed to reduce the levels of circulating calcitriol.

Some risk factors, including your genetic background and nutritional disadvantages you may have experienced as a child, are beyond your control, and the medications you must take may not offer much choice either. But there *are* steps you can take to improve your status in the matter of osteoporosis risk. You can certainly avoid overindulging in alcohol. You can forgo smoking—which, as you know, you should do in any event, for multiple health reasons. Above all, you can make an effort to deliver adequate supplies of the essential element your bones need.

## Get More Calcium

There is no question: Calcium is the key to preventing osteoporosis. And logic dictates that the earlier the awareness of that fact the better. The more bone mass built up by the time of the peak period, the greater the continuing strength of one's bones and the greater the protection from osteoporosis.

There is disagreement on how much calcium most people require, and individual needs may differ. In 1984, the U.S. National Institutes of Health (NIH) said that all women should get 1000 to 1500 milligrams (mg) per day. In 1989, the National Academy of Sciences set the recommended daily allowance (RDA) at 1200 mg per day for ages eleven to twenty-four and 800 mg thereafter. A 1990 international symposium on osteoporosis concluded that 800 mg was a good minimum for everyone.

At this writing, NIH suggests 1000 mg daily, except: 1200 mg if you're under age twenty-five (and not pregnant or breast-feeding a baby);* 2000 mg if you're eighteen or younger and pregnant or breast-feeding; 1400 mg if you're nineteen or older and pregnant or breast-feeding; 1500 mg if you've reached or passed menopause and are not taking estrogen. (The age of twenty-five is when more than 90 percent of peak bone mass has been attained—although, as I mentioned earlier, it will keep increasing for another decade.) Where you fit into this scheme is best discussed with your own physician.

Research over the past decade has also suggested that adequate, or even extra, calcium may be helpful to one's health in other ways, in addition to osteoporosis prevention. Several studies have shown an inverse relationship between blood pressure and calcium in hypertensive people—that is, the higher the calcium intake, the lower the pressure (an effect not seen in subjects whose blood pressure is normal in the first place). Some investigators have suggested that increased calcium may play some protective role against cancer of the colon. Calcium has also been reported to lower the likelihood of premature childbirth. (A study is currently in progress, under the auspices of the National Institutes of Health, assessing this possibility as well as calcium's potential for reducing the risk of hypertension in pregnancy.)

Where do you get calcium? Nutritionists agree that, in general, the best source for all nutrients is the natural one: the diet. The best dietary sources of calcium, as you doubtless know, are

---

*In pregnancy, calcium is needed for the bones and teeth of the developing fetus. In breast-feeding, calcium is required for milk production. In both cases, those needs will automatically be met, and the mother's bone-stored supply will be depleted.

milk and other dairy foods—cheeses, ice cream, yogurt,[*] and so on. And the good news is that those dairy foods that are best for you otherwise are also the best sources of calcium, while such high-fat dairy products as butter, cream, and cream cheese have relatively low calcium content.

As you may not know, there are other good diet sources of calcium, too. Three ounces of canned sardines (in oil, with bones), for example, provides 370 mg of calcium. Ten dried figs will give you 270 mg. An average slice of pizza (an eighth of a 15-inch pie) offers 220 mg. Three ounces of canned salmon contains 165 mg. A packet of fortified instant oatmeal supplies 160 mg, as does a cup of tomato soup made with milk. Green leafy vegetables, such as collards and kale, are also rich in calcium (a medium broccoli spear, cooked and drained, has more than 200 mg), and some fruit juices and breads are calcium-fortified. Tofu and other soybean products are good sources as well.

But it may be impossible for any number of reasons—including calorie restrictions and other health considerations, as well as personal tastes—to meet your calcium needs with diet alone. You can also get calcium through supplements. Such supplements are available without prescription, in several forms, both brand-named and generic, including calcium carbonate, calcium citrate, calcium gluconate, and calcium lactate. Research has shown that calcium citrate is particularly effective

---

[*] Some people are lactose-intolerant, meaning they can't digest milk sugar and suffer serious stomach upsets from most dairy foods. Yogurt may be a feasible alternative. Lactase tablets, containing the digestive enzyme that lactose-intolerant persons lack, are also available.

because of its high absorption levels compared with some other forms, which may be more dependent on the pH (acid–alkaline) balance in different parts of the gastrointestinal tract. Taking supplements with food increases their absorption by the intestine.

You should know, however, that the quality of calcium supplements is not regulated by law. If the calcium in the calcium pills you take never reaches your bones, you may as well not be taking them. Perform a simple test: Drop a pill in some ordinary vinegar. If it doesn't dissolve within half an hour, it won't dissolve in your GI tract, either.

Will extra vitamin D, by itself or along with the calcium, help? Not necessarily. Calcitriol (the active form of vitamin D) supplementation combined with calcium supplements has been found useful in preventing hip fractures in the elderly (people in their seventies and eighties and up), in whom deficiency is not uncommon. Vitamin deficiency is less likely earlier in life, and studies in younger postmenopausal women have shown conflicting results.

A New Zealand study reported in 1992, however, appeared to demonstrate superiority of calcitriol (alone) over calcium (alone) in preventing fractures. All the subjects in the study were postmenopausal women (aged fifty to seventy-nine) who had already suffered vertebral compression fractures. Those in the calcium group received the supplement in the form of calcium gluconate; it's possible that with calcium carbonate or calcium citrate, the forms most used in this country, the results might have been different.

Various other foods can interfere with your body's calcium balance, whether the calcium comes from your diet, from supplements, or both. Some foods do so by lowering the level of calcium absorption. One such group of foods are those containing chemicals called oxalates, which form an insoluble substance in combination with calcium; spinach, cabbage, chocolate, cocoa, nuts, and tea are especially high in oxalates. High quantities of dietary fat—as well as too-high quantities of otherwise-good-for-you fiber—can also decrease calcium absorption.

Diets unusually high in protein, sodium (as in table salt), or caffeine (three or more cups of coffee a day, or the equivalent in tea or cola drinks) can cause depletion of the body's calcium levels by increasing excretion of the mineral.

Other supplements and drugs, besides corticosteroids, may encourage a tendency to osteoporosis. Megadoses of zinc supplements or vitamin A can decrease calcium absorption, as can some antacids containing aluminum (antacids containing calcium, though, can do double duty as calcium supplements). A variety of medications—including some sedatives, muscle relaxants, anticonvulsants, and oral drugs for diabetes—can inactivate the calcitriol needed for bone rebuilding. And certain types of diuretics (drugs that reduce fluid buildup) can deprive the body of calcium by speeding its excretion.

A precaution: If you have had kidney stones—that term covers stones anywhere in the urinary tract—it's important for you to talk with your doctor before you take any calcium supplement. There are a number of distinct types of kidney stones, and some contain calcium. People who have a tendency to form calcium-containing stones should discuss their calcium intake with their physicians.

For updated information about calcium, in foods and in supplements, you can call the Calcium Information Center, a component of the Nutrition Information Center affiliated with New York Hospital-Cornell Medical Center; the toll-free number is (800) 321-2681.

## Alternative/Additional Medicine

If you've been taking calcium supplements and bone scanning nevertheless reveals a continuing problem, your physician may suggest other recourses. One is the thyroid hormone I mentioned earlier, calcitonin or thyrocalcitonin. This hormone acts to slow bone loss by reducing the rate of resorption. Clinical trials suggest that it acts somewhat selectively, though—that it's very effective in decreasing spinal bone loss and preventing vertebral fractures, less so in preventing bone loss in arms and legs.

Until recently, calcitonin was available only in injectable form; the injection is subcutaneous (just under the skin) and given every day or every other day. The hormone is now also marketed in intranasal (nose spray) form.

The calcitonin used in this country, derived from salmon, can cause allergic reactions in some people. If your physician believes the hormone may be helpful for you, skin tests may be advisable before treatment is begun, especially if you have a history of allergies, as many lupus patients do. It should also be noted that some people become "resistant" to its benefits because they produce antibodies against it, although this is less likely to occur with the intranasal form.

A drug called etidronate (Didronel), which is taken orally, also decreases bone resorption, specifically by inhibiting osteoclast activity. Long used in the treatment of other bone conditions, etidronate has also recently been tried for treatment of osteoporosis, specifically in postmenopausal women. One of the early studies found that high doses, in addition to decreasing bone resorption, also interfered with mineralization of new bone. Lower doses, however, have proved helpful, reducing resorption without adversely affecting new bone. *Note:* This drug must always be taken on an empty stomach.

Etidronate is one of a class of drugs called biphosphonates. Another biphosphonate, pamidronate, was approved by the U.S. Food and Drug Administration in 1991, specifically for intravenous injection in the treatment of hypercalcemia (excessive calcium circulating in the bloodstream) associated with certain forms of cancer. It is also under investigation, however, for a number of other conditions, including osteoporosis (by oral administration). Thus far, it appears to be a more powerful inhibitor of bone resorption than etidronate, and osteoporotic patients have experienced a gain in bone mass. Other biphosphonates are being explored as well.

How about fluoride? Since it is a highly effective strengthener of teeth, defending them against decay caused by bacteria-produced acids—might it have a similarly beneficial impact on bone? That thought has indeed occurred to researchers in this area. Thus far, though, the results of their studies have not been promising.

It was found in clinical trials with postmenopausal women who had suffered vertebral fractures that fluoride in fairly high doses did increase bone density—and also the number of new fractures; the treatment seemed to create new bone that was dense but structurally abnormal. Fluoride in lower doses doesn't appear to be a viable alternative. In one recent study there was an increased incidence of hip fractures among elderly people in areas with fluoridated water.

Clinical researchers at the University of Texas Southwestern Medical Center in Dallas reported in 1991 that a different approach, using a slow-release form of fluoride combined with calcium citrate, had proved helpful in a small group of patients, with confirmed improvement in both bone density and bone strength. That trial was uncontrolled, however (there was no untreated group for comparison), and the research team is, at this writing, engaged in a larger, controlled study.

## The Benefits of Exercise

Finally, there is one anti-osteoporosis regimen I can recommend without reservation: regular exercise—particularly weight-bearing exercise. Whatever other preventive steps are taken, the addition of regular exercise will without question be helpful.

Quite a few studies have definitely demonstrated the direct relationship between exercise and bone mass—and bone mass, we know, is the main factor in reducing the potential for fracture-fostering osteoporosis. While the nature of this association isn't fully understood, it appears that in the course of exercise the muscle activity exerts a kinetic effect on the bone to which it's attached, an effect that stimulates osteoblastic activity—that is, the formation of new bone. Conversely, it's been observed that in periods of enforced immobility—when long bed rest has been necessary, for example—a rise in the rate of bone resorption takes place.

Indeed, a recent discovery hints that this factor may play a significant role in the history of osteoporosis. Many observers have noticed an increase in osteoporotic fractures over the years, an increase that's age-specific (so not attributable to the use of corticosteroids) but not accounted for by the fact that people live longer these days. Perhaps there's another reason.

A recent London church restoration required digging up the remains of parishioners buried during the eighteenth and early nineteenth centuries. Their ages at the time of death were all known. When scientists, curious about changes over time, scanned the femurs (thighbones) of female skeletons from the churchyard and compared them with those of present-day women of comparable age, they found distinct differences in rate of bone loss. It was much higher in the modern women, even prior to menopause (in fact, in the exhumed bones, there had been *no* significant premenopausal loss).

The investigators' 1993 report, noting that the difference could be due to many factors, nevertheless remarked that the women of that area, called Spitalfields, were known to have done a great deal of walking and to have worked up to fourteen to sixteen hours a day at the main local occupation, silk-weaving (in addition to caring for their children). One factor in accounting for the difference, the researchers concluded, could be a decrease in physical activity.

In any event, we know that loss of muscle strength, which occurs mainly through inactivity, contributes directly to loss of bone strength. Improve muscle strength, through exercise, and you improve bone strength as well.

Weight-bearing exercise, especially, leads to increased muscular strength. That term doesn't refer only to literally lifting weights (i.e., dumbbells); it denotes any activity in which weight is lifted or carried, including kneebends, stair-climbing, dancing, and just plain walking. Much "aerobic" exercise promoted for cardiovascular and overall health qualifies in this area as well. Generally, a program of moderate exercise that addresses both concerns, and provides activity for all the skeletal muscles, is the best choice for everyone.

The American Academy of Orthopaedic Surgeons (AAOS) strongly recommends walking as a basic daily activity in a program to prevent osteoporosis, noting that, in addition to strengthening leg muscles, it peps up circulation. Start with a short walk, such as a quarter of a mile or about five city blocks, increasing the distance gradually over a period of weeks, until a routine one mile a day is reached. The Academy cautions that overexertion should be avoided, and that if any discomfort or breathlessness occurs, medical consultation is in order. I would add that walkers should also heed local air pollution alerts, since outdoor physical exertion under those circumstances can be hazardous to your health; do your strolling indoors on days like that.

Here is a simple exercise program adapted from one developed by the President's Council on Physical Fitness and recommended by the AAOS. Designed originally as a beginning program for people over age sixty, it can serve as a good start for anyone unused to very much strenuous activity. The "level 1" routines are the easiest, and you should feel comfortable with them, and able to accomplish them all without difficulty, before you add the "level 2" exercises (from that point on, perform all ten at each exercise session). Similarly, try the more challenging "level 3" exercises only after you've mastered those at the previous level; then, go through all fourteen routines each day.

Three precautions, before you begin:

1. If you've had any arthritis, other joint problem, or fracture, or if scanning has shown that you have any degree of osteoporosis, get your physician's approval first. Especially if you have suffered an injury, rehabilitative physical therapy may be recommended before you undertake any new physical activity.

2. Pay no attention to the "no pain, no gain" adage. Slight soreness, which may persist overnight—or even appear the next day rather than immediately—is not unusual when a previously inactive muscle is exercised. *Pain* is something different. It is a message from your body that something is

amiss, a signal to stop what you are doing and check with your doctor.

3. If you develop any new symptoms, or any aspect of your lupus worsens, stop the program *and* make a date with your physician. The problem may or may not be related to the exercise. If it is, it's important to clarify the connection. If it isn't, you need to find out what *is* causing it.

# Level 1

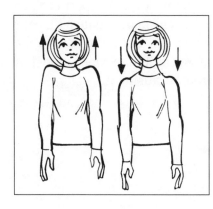

1a: Start with this simple shrug, repeating it ten times. Important: Stand straight, keep your head perfectly erect, and be careful not to lift one shoulder higher than the other (stand in front of a mirror to make sure).

1b: Choose a straight chair, and slide forward until you're sitting on the edge of the seat. Lift one leg, from the hip, until it's straight out, parallel to the floor. Hold it there for a slow count of three (later, if this seems too easy, you can increase the count to five or more), then lower it, as slowly as you can, to rest your foot on the floor. Do the same with the other leg. Repeat the full routine five times to start; later, increase to ten or fifteen times. Be sure to protect your lower back from strain by consciously using your abdominal muscles (this precaution is important with routines *1e* and *1f* as well).

Illustrations by Bill Kresse

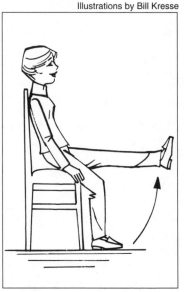

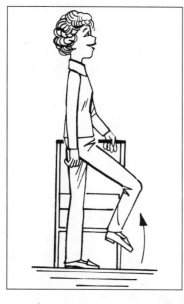

1c: Hold on to a chair back, porch railing, counter, or other convenient support, and, standing perfectly straight, raise one knee as high as you can, hold for a slow count of three, and lower. Do this a total of five times (later, you can increase to ten), then repeat with the other leg.

1d: Sit in a straight chair again, but this time, sit up straight, with your back against the back of the chair, your knees bent; your feet should rest comfortably on the floor. This exercise is like *1b*, *except* that your leg moves only from the knee down, coming up to form a straight line with your thigh.

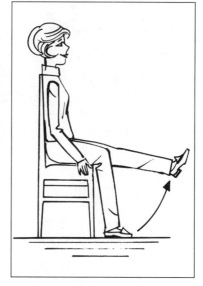

1e: Holding on to a chair or other support with both hands, raise one leg behind you, as high as you can. Important: Keep the leg straight (you should feel the pull through your buttocks, not the back of your knee), and *stand erect*, shoulders back and head up; don't tilt forward. Do ten times with each leg; you can do ten raises with one leg and then ten with the other, or alternate legs, as you like.

1f: Stand erect, again holding on to a support with both hands. Keeping your heels on the floor and your torso erect, bend your knees to approach a "sitting" position; go as far as possible. Return to standing position as slowly as you can. Perform this exercise ten times.

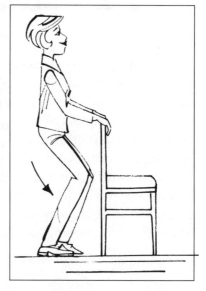

# Level 2

2a: Two- to three-pound weights are suggested for this exercise; you can use household objects, such as cans of food, but weights are standardized and a great deal easier to grip firmly, so they won't slip out of your grasp. Stand erect and hold the weights at your sides, either palms forward (as shown) or palms toward your body as if holding a briefcase, whichever's more comfortable. Bend your arms to curl the weights upward; if you've begun in the second described position, allow your wrists to turn on the way up, palms toward you. Repeat ten to fifteen times, increasing later to twenty or more.

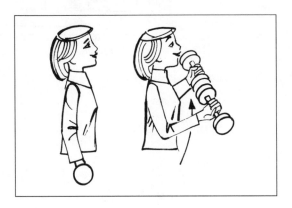

2b: Start by kneeling as shown, hands placed at shoulder width but slightly forward, arms straight. Slowly bend your arms to lower your upper body until your nose touches the floor. Important: *Don't* let your forearms rest on the floor. Return to the starting position by straightening your arms to lift your torso. Repeat ten times or more.

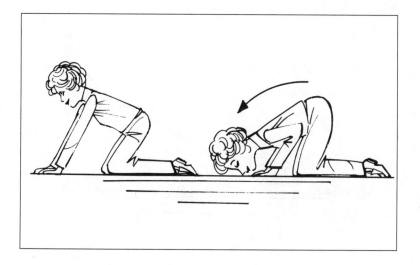

2c: Lie on one side as shown, perfectly straight, tilting neither forward nor back. Slowly raise the upper leg, keeping it straight and aligned with your body (i.e., neither forward nor backward but toward the ceiling); it may be helpful to have someone else tell you if you're performing this one correctly. Repeat at least ten times, then turn over to the other side and do the same with the other leg.

2d:  Start this routine by standing with feet very slightly apart, hands on hips. Slide one leg forward, bending that knee as far as you can, at the same time swinging your arms straight forward; the heel of the other leg must remain on the floor, and the back leg and the upper part of your body should form a straight line. Perform five times with each leg, later increasing to ten.

# Level 3

3a: These arm curls use heavier weights—five-pounders are suggested to start—and, since simultaneous lifting (at least at first) is likely to throw off posture and balance, alternate lifts are used: Bring one weight up to your shoulder; then, as you lower that one to your side, raise the other one, continuing to alternate until you've performed the full routine at

least ten times with each arm. When you feel more confident, you can try simultaneous lifting.

3b: This is the same as 1a, except that now you're lifting weights as you shrug your shoulders. Start with five-pound weights; try eight-pounders later, if you feel up to it.

3c: For this routine, stand straight, a five-pound weight in each hand, feet shoulder width apart. Slowly rise up on your toes as high as you can, and hold as long as you can do so without losing your balance. Slowly lower your heels to the floor. Repeat ten times. Variation: Try performing with your toes turned slightly outward, like a ballet dancer (rotate your leg from the hip).

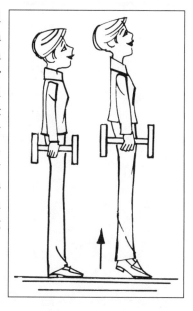

3d: Start as you did for the last exercise, standing straight, weights in your hands, feet about shoulder width apart. Slowly bend your knees—keeping your heels on the floor—as far as you can while maintaining your balance and your torso erect. Then, as slowly as you can, straighten your legs to return to standing position. Repeat ten times.

# CHAPTER
# 9

# A Prudent Approach to Pregnancy

It has long been known that pregnancy can be problematic for many lupus patients. To begin with, many find it difficult to conceive. And if they do succeed in becoming pregnant, the outlook—statistically, at least—is not heartening.

It's estimated that between 10 and 15 percent of all confirmed pregnancies end in spontaneous abortion (miscarriage); among women with lupus, the figure has been 25 to 30 percent. Some 10 percent of all babies born in our country arrive prematurely; among women with lupus the risk is three times as high. In other words, based on numbers alone, the chance of successful full-term pregnancy would seem to be 50 percent or less.

There are differences from hospital to hospital, though (whether these variations are based on patient or medical-care factors isn't clear). The Lupus Pregnancy Center at Johns

Hopkins University, which is a continuing project and sees patients at least monthly—routine pregnancy evaluations, as well as lupus assessments—reported the following update in 1992: Fifty-one pregnancies had been followed to completion. Eight ended in miscarriage; nineteen of the forty-three babies born (44 percent) arrived prematurely. The researchers observed that hypertension appeared to be a significant factor in prematurity.

At one time, there was general agreement that lupus absolutely precluded childbearing, and that if conception occurred, therapeutic abortion should be performed.

## High Risk, Low Risk

That thinking has changed, radically. The foregoing figures have been gathered from a number of reported studies in lupus patients. Further study has shown that not all patients are at equal risk. Some are doubtless wise to avoid conceiving a child. Others, however, can probably contemplate pregnancy with few qualms (though not, as I shall point out, without sensible precautions). And the physician can now offer some guidance to help the patient make this important decision.

Correlations of certain maternal characteristics with pregnancy outcomes over the years have provided a great deal of information. Seriously impaired kidney function, or impaired function of any other major organ or system, is not a good omen for successful pregnancy. Severe flare of disease during a pregnancy that began in remission suggests that the same thing may occur again, in future pregnancies—although other factors, of course, may have accounted for the prior episode, not excluding inappropriate or inadequate medication or another aspect of health care.

A state of complete remission at the time of conception *and* for the prior six months (at least) has a better prognosis for success, while active disease at the time of conception is statistically associated with a higher incidence of complications and adverse outcomes.

Further clarification has come with the recent recognition of the relevance of a family of antibodies called anti-phospholipids, or APLs. They are antibodies against substances found universally in the membranes of cells. While their existence has been known for several decades, it was not until the late 1980s that the significance of APLs in lupus generally, and in pregnancy in particular, began to be appreciated.

It should be noted that the antibodies in question are not exclusive to lupus and play no part in diagnosing the disease. We now believe that 1 or 2 percent of the general population (and higher proportions of those with autoimmune disorders) have these antibodies. I also want to stress that they are not necessarily predictive of serious conditions; they have been found in many people, with and without lupus, who may not develop any critical medical problems.

One clue to the presence of APLs is the false-positive syphilis testing I mentioned in chapter 2. While it is one of the elements considered in diagnosing lupus, people without lupus may also test falsely positive for syphilis. A false-positive syphilis test, by itself, is not predictive of what may happen in pregnancy. Nor does it necessarily suggest the presence of *other* APLs, although there is what some researchers call a "loose" correlation.

Two specific APLs have emerged in research reports as especially significant in lupus and in pregnancy. Both may be detected by blood tests. Both are associated with circulatory problems and with fetal loss.

One is called anti-cardiolipin (ACL), and it reacts particularly with the phospholipids of cells lining blood vessels. It has been linked to a variety of unexpected incidents generally, including heart attacks and strokes in young people; phlebitis; the development of certain heart-valve abnormalities; thrombocytopenia; and in pregnancy, recurrent miscarriages or fetal death, associated with abnormal (fetal) heart rate, in the second trimester. ("Ordinary" miscarriages, often traceable to developmental mishaps, typically take place earlier; lupus patients have a somewhat higher incidence in the first trimester as well.) The risk of fetal loss in those with this antibody has been estimated to be close to 60 percent.

Two Israeli researchers reported in 1992 on an experiment in which they injected ACL antibodies from lupus patients into pregnant mice (not the mouse strains with the equivalent of lupus I've mentioned elsewhere, but ordinary, healthy mice). The mice developed thrombocytopenia and experienced increased fetal loss. And, the researchers added, the same thing happened to mice injected with ACL from persons who did *not* have lupus.

ACL is found, at one time or another, in about one-third of people with lupus. They often have what has been termed "atypical" lupus, lupus that doesn't quite fit the American College of Rheumatology diagnostic criteria, and they may test negative for ANA.

The second significant APL is called lupus anticoagulant (LAC); it's found in about a tenth of lupus patients. Its name would seem to suggest that it prevents coagulation (clotting) of blood, signaling a tendency to hemorrhage. Indeed, its presence is signaled by an assay (called the partial thromboplastin time, or PTT, test) that shows clotting time to be prolonged.

But the name, despite the test, is misleading. LAC in real life is almost never associated with excessive bleeding. On the contrary: The link is with an inclination, in some people with the antibody, to form obstructive clots, or thrombi, especially in veins (venous thrombosis), sometimes associated with pulmonary emboli, fragments of these clots which lodge in the lungs. In pregnancy, LAC has been linked to miscarriage or stillbirth due to thrombi in the placenta; again, the loss typically takes place in mid-pregnancy.

It's quite possible that Connie, who experienced severe circulatory complications—specifically, thrombophlebitis and pulmonary emboli—in one pregnancy and was advised not to attempt a second (see chapter 1), would have tested positive for one of these antibodies, had such testing been done when she was contemplating pregnancy. That was not to happen, however, for another decade.

Overall, in women who have suffered unexplained repeated miscarriages, various studies have found APLs in proportions ranging from 8 to 42 percent, while the reported prevalence of these antibodies in groups of obstetric patients in general has ranged from zero to 10 percent. (ACL has been more consistently related to fetal loss than LAC.) Clearly, there is a significant connection.

Just as clearly, since APLs are found in only a minority of women who have had recurrent miscarriages, they can't be blamed for all failed pregnancies. Nor do they completely explain the higher probability of premature delivery, or of certain other pregnancy complications, in women with lupus.

Now, let's take a look at the mutual impact of pregnancy on lupus and of lupus on pregnancy—not only the APL-associated perils but others as well. We'll also consider what should be done, when pregnancy is undertaken, to minimize the risks—and meet the challenges—to both mother and baby.

## Planning Ahead

I've singled out particular hazards—but it's generally wise, if you have lupus and decide to have a baby, to view it as a high-risk undertaking. That term, in this context, doesn't mean an assumption that something will go amiss. It means that all possible precautions should be taken and that problems may nevertheless occur and should be anticipated.

Safeguards recommended for every pregnancy should be taken especially seriously, from the moment you know you want to conceive (don't wait until the pregnancy is confirmed): Don't drink alcohol, or smoke, or use any other "recreational" drugs—or, for that matter, any medicinal substances unless they're prescribed or suggested by your doctor. Do eat a well-balanced diet, follow directions for medications, and see your rheumatologist and your obstetrician regularly.

The latter should be a specialist with extensive experience in managing high-risk pregnancies, preferably in lupus patients; should be in close touch with your rheumatologist; and should want to see you *much* more frequently than pregnant women are usually checked on, especially after the first three months—which may mean several times a week during the second and third trimesters.

Don't even *think* about home birth, or even childbirth at a freestanding "birthing center." The latter has often proved to be an appropriate and even ideal setting for an uncomplicated, risk-free delivery under the care of an experienced nurse-midwife, but these centers are intended *only* for such deliveries.

A woman with lupus (or, for that matter, any other chronic condition that poses the slightest risk to the well-being of mother or child) should plan for delivery to take place at a hospital. The hospital should be one that is equipped to care for premature or otherwise distressed infants or has ready access to such a facility—not because anything *will* go wrong, but just in *case* something does.

Because lupus has been known to flare following childbirth, it's a good idea to plan ahead for that contingency as well. Make arrangements for alternative or assistant child care during the immediate postpartum period.

You should also be aware of two recent precautions regarding pregnancy, applying to women both with and without lupus. In 1992, the U.S. Public Health Service issued a general advisory recommending that all women of childbearing age who might possibly become pregnant take 0.4 milligrams of folic acid each day. This B vitamin has been shown to help reduce the risk of neural-tube defects (NTDs), malformations of the fetal brain and/or spinal cord. The reason for taking the vitamin even if you haven't become pregnant is that the fetal defects can occur in the first month, before pregnancy has even been confirmed.

A word, in connection with this subject, on a particular kind of testing during pregnancy. There is a substance called alpha-fetoprotein (AFP), produced mainly by the fetal liver and not found in any significant quantity in the blood of adults. A test for AFP is routinely performed on an expectant mother's blood at about the fourteenth to sixteenth week of pregnancy. While a somewhat heightened AFP level is expected and normal, unusually high concentrations are statistically associated with (though by no means *proof* of) NTDs.

If high AFP levels are found, further testing is performed in an effort to find the reason. Broad surveys involving thousands of pregnancies boil down the data this way: About 40 percent of raised AFP levels are actually found to reflect NTDs; in a bit more than a quarter of the cases, other abnormal fetal conditions are present; and in about one-third, the babies are perfectly normal.

These figures may not hold for lupus patients, however. In an interesting study reported in 1992, the Maryland State Health Department followed a cohort of pregnant women, both with and without lupus, performed AFP testing, and correlated those findings with pregnancy outcome. High AFP levels were found in 7.4 percent of the lupus patients, versus only 2.6 percent of the control (non-lupus) subjects—nearly triple the rate. This higher proportion was associated *not* with a higher incidence of babies with defects, but with a higher likelihood of premature birth; it was also associated with the mother's taking higher doses of prednisone.

The second advisory for pregnant women in general, from the Food and Drug Administration, concerns ACE (angiotensin-converting-enzyme) inhibitors, a group of drugs used to treat hypertension (high blood pressure). These agents, the FDA has warned, can cause serious or even fatal fetal damage if they're taken during the second and third trimesters (the last six months) of pregnancy. Brand names of these drugs, at this writing, include Accupril, Altace, Capoten, Capozide, Lotensin, Monopril, Prinivil, Prinzide, Vaseretic, Vasotec, Zestoretic, and Zestril. If you're pregnant and taking one of these drugs: *Don't panic,* and *don't stop* the medication on your own; that could trigger even more problems, for both mother and child. What to do: Contact the physician who prescribed the drug, who can select an effective alternative.

## On the Alert

Throughout pregnancy, monitoring must be done, with close tabs kept on both lupus activity and fetal progress. Medications may be added and subtracted to keep the disease under the best possible control, especially to treat nephritis (kidney inflammation) and other similarly serious developments.

If you've been pregnant before and you miscarried, or you have a history of blood clots, your doctor will probably want to test for those trouble-making anti-phospholipid antibodies, if such testing hasn't already been done; he or she may want to do so even in the absence of prior problems. Two or more tests several weeks apart may be performed in order to confirm the results.

If there seems to be a definite risk of your developing clots that will threaten you and/or the fetus, special prophylactic measures may be taken. During the period of heaviest risk, in mid-pregnancy, prednisone dosage adjustments may be required. Or prevention may take the form of "blood-thinning" medication—perhaps something as simple as a daily dose of baby aspirin; or an injected drug such as heparin may be recommended. There is not yet, at this writing, complete agreement on which of these measures may be superior to another. Preliminary results of trials of low-dose prednisone plus aspirin in patients with APLs seem promising for reducing the incidence of miscarriage.

Another critical threat is a condition called *preeclampsia*, or sometimes *toxemia of pregnancy* (a misnomer; there is no toxin involved). The complication occurs in 5 to 7 percent of all pregnancies in this country—but in lupus patients, the rate is perhaps 20 percent.

This condition is signaled by a rise in blood pressure and/or proteinuria, and this is one of the reasons frequent physician visits, with pressure checks and urinalyses, are vital; preeclampsia is virtually symptomless, except that there may be some fluid retention, with swelling around fingers and ankles, and slightly greater than expected weight gain. Any of these signs and symptoms can suggest other problems, including a lupus flare, which underscores the importance of having an experienced physician following the patient throughout pregnancy.

Preeclampsia strikes in the latter months of pregnancy and is considered a major threat to both mother and baby if it progresses. Hospitalization is generally in order, with the baby delivered as quickly as possible, which may mean necessary induction of labor or cesarean section despite likely prematurity, since prematurity is the lesser hazard under these circumstances. (Sometimes this complication arises extremely late in pregnancy, close to the expected delivery date.)

Of course, in addition to constant monitoring of the mother's health, the baby-to-be is closely observed as well, to assure normal growth and development and continuing vital signs. Sonograms—ultrasound visualizations—along with heartbeat monitoring attest to fetal progress. Monitoring is especially intense after the fetus becomes viable—able to survive outside the womb—at about the twenty-fourth to twenty-sixth week of pregnancy.

Actually, as soon as fetal movement has started (most women become aware of these movements by about the eighteenth or twentieth week), the woman herself is an important monitor. As pregnancy progresses into the sixth and seventh months, most mothers-to-be develop a familiarity with their baby's characteristic movements. Any slowing or other change in these movements may mean trouble and should be reported to the doctor immediately, since speedy delivery can sometimes rescue an infant threatened by incipient failure of placental circulation.

In some instances, how to proceed when fetal distress—or potential distress—is deemed to be a possibility can be a very close judgment call. On the one hand, removing the baby prematurely from the relative safety of the womb to the harsh environment outside cannot be contemplated lightly. But neither can continued exposure to antibodies that may be damaging the infant's heart. The balance is a delicate one, and the decision must be made by an experienced physician *and* an informed patient.

## Meanwhile, About Mom's Lupus . . .

Although there are exceptions, in the majority of cases there is unlikely to be a worsening of lupus during pregnancy; studies have shown that exacerbations occur in only a minority. Most of the complications we've mentioned seem to be due more to pregnancy than to lupus. Rashes may erupt temporarily, but that's not considered serious.

More likely is flare following childbirth. That's possibly related to hormonal realignments, especially the sudden drop in progesterone, the ovarian/placental hormone that has helped to sustain pregnancy.(There may also be an *apparent* spurt of postpartum hair loss. It's actually unrelated to lupus and reflects an increased growth of hair during pregnancy with a subsequent return to normal.)

In general, most medications taken regularly will be continued during pregnancy and will not harm the fetus. If steroids are needed, prednisone or prednisolone is generally preferred, since the way these drugs are metabolized in the placenta limits the amount that reaches the baby. (Some other corticosteroids cross that barrier intact and are used only if an effect on the baby is deliberately intended. One is dexamethasone, which may be given to the mother when premature birth is imminent, since it has been found to speed fetal lung maturity and help to prevent serious respiratory problems in the newborn.) Hydroxychloroquine and other antimalarials, as well as

143

such potent immunosuppressants as azathioprine and cyclo-phosphamide, are generally avoided in pregnancy if possible.

As I mentioned in chapter 7, one adverse effect of steroids can be osteoporosis—generally after lengthy therapy. Pregnancy, however, poses a special risk: The fetus needs calcium for bone development, and that can cause depletion in the mother's own supply, increasing the possibility of bone problems. If the mother-to-be is taking corticosteroids, calcium supplementation may be advised. See chapter 8 for a full discussion of this risk.

To counter possible postpartum problems, some physicians feel that it's a good idea to increase the mother's dosage of corticosteroids about the time she goes into labor, keeping it high for several weeks thereafter and then gradually tapering it. Others disagree. They feel these drugs should be given or increased (if already being taken) only in response to disease activity, not for prophylaxis. My own feeling is that no preconceived "rule" should be followed and that therapy should be completely individualized—erring, when in doubt, on the side of less medication rather than more.

Drug considerations in breast-feeding—medications do find their way into the nursing mother's milk, albeit in very small amounts—are similar to those in pregnancy, although both rheumatologist and pediatrician should be consulted about the safety of the specific drug(s) being taken.

Antimalarials are particularly persistent and pose some risk of eye damage to the infant, just as they do in the mother, so nursing when taking these drugs isn't a good idea. High-dose salicylate therapy can pose a risk of bleeding problems. Other NSAIDs may vary in safety, since some accumulate in the body more than others. While low-to-moderate doses of corticosteroids seem to be compatible with breast-feeding, it's probably best to limit nursing to times when maternal levels are lowest (before the morning dose and in the evening), giving formula at other times; the consensus is that breast-feeding is best avoided if high doses of steroids are being taken.

In most circumstances, breast-feeding—at least to some degree—is possible and desirable, since pediatric authorities agree that breast milk is best for the baby. Prematurity, incidentally, does not preclude providing a baby with breast milk, which can be expressed for feeding in the intensive-care nursery; if an infant is too immature to suck and must at first be nourished intravenously, milk can still be pumped and frozen for later use. (Don't thaw it by high-temperature microwaving; that's been shown to diminish its valuable infection-fighting properties.)

## Will the Baby Be Okay?

The highest potential risk to the baby is the possibility of premature arrival. As noted earlier, in women with lupus, the statistics tell us there's a 30 percent chance of premature childbirth.

A full-term pregnancy is defined as one that lasts from thirty-seven to forty-two weeks, so that any baby born before thirty-seven weeks is called premature. In fact, a baby born after thirty-five weeks is typically fine, except for not-quite-ready temperature controls, which may mean just a couple of days in an incubator.

Babies born earlier than that generally have some problems and are cared for in a neonatal intensive-care unit. Those problems may vary. Treatment may include measures to deal with respiratory distress, to provide adequate nutrition when a baby cannot yet suck (intravenous feeding may be needed if the digestive system is not yet operating normally), and to cope with other aspects of immaturity. Babies weighing in at three pounds or more generally do quite well; in fact, some infants weighing not much over a pound at birth have survived and grown to be bright, healthy children.

I've said that lupus isn't directly inherited, and the disease isn't transmitted from mother to baby. There is, however, a small incidence, among babies born to lupus patients, of a lupus-related syndrome. It appears to stem from antibodies that cross the placenta and is associated chiefly with anti-Ro antibodies; one very broad European study, reported at a 1992 international conference on lupus, found *all* cases of the syndrome occurring in mothers with anti-Ro antibodies. As I noted in chapter 2, about 30 percent of lupus patients overall have these antibodies. About 10 to 20 percent of them—that is, about 3 to 6 percent of women with lupus—will give birth to babies with "neonatal lupus." (After having one such child, the chances of a woman's having subsequent children with the condition are about one in four.)

Neonatal lupus, unlike "regular" lupus, is not lasting. It consists of a transient rash and transient abnormalities in blood tests (they have usually disappeared by six to eight months of age) and may also include a condition known as congenital heart block; in various studies, the latter has been present in half or fewer of neonatal lupus cases. "Heart block" may sound as if the heart comes to a halt. It doesn't. The phrase is a medical term for misfiring of certain electrical signals within the heart, resulting in heartbeat irregularities, occasionally serious enough to require a pacemaker.

A series of published studies examining specific antibodies in women with lupus who had given birth to babies with congenital heart block found anti-Ro antibodies in 98 percent; in some studies, the figure was 100 percent. There is also a lesser association with anti-La antibodies, which were reported in

86 percent of the patients studied. The investigators also tested groups of control patients—mothers who had been diagnosed with lupus, Sjögren's syndrome, or nonspecific connective-tissue disease, and who delivered babies who did not suffer from heart block. Among these women, anti-Ro and anti-La antibodies were identified in, respectively, 33 percent and 15 percent.

In a study at New York University Medical Center, reported at an American College of Rheumatology meeting in late 1992, all of a series of mothers with heart-block babies were found to have anti-Ro antibodies; 80 percent had anti-La antibodies as well—figures in line with those previously cited. Some of the women had subsequent pregnancies; 21 percent of their offspring were also born with heart block. (Some of the women in this study had been diagnosed with lupus at the time of their pregnancy, others with Sjögren's syndrome; still others had neither condition.)

One London clinic, in an attempt to calculate risks on the basis of antibodies, has estimated that 20 percent of women with anti-Ro antibodies may deliver a baby with neonatal lupus. What factors distinguish those who run a higher risk from the others is not known.

## The Question of Contraception

Many lupus patients, like many other women, will choose to avoid pregnancy, whether because of potential complications or because of personal choice. If you're one of them, what contraceptive method should you choose?

There's a clear consensus that oral contraceptives ("the Pill"), which are hormones, are best avoided, since they pose a heightened risk of such circulatory problems as high blood pressure, vasculitis (blood-vessel inflammation), and thrombosis. Lupus patients are already at higher-than-average risk of these conditions; it doesn't make sense to raise the odds. The Pill has also been known to cause exacerbations of lupus.

It's my feeling that, while experience with them has been more limited, other hormonal contraceptives—such as levonorgestrel implants (Norplant)—at least theoretically pose similar risks, and I'd advise against them.

Intrauterine devices, IUDs, are also best avoided, because of the possibility of perforation, bleeding, or pelvic infection. Those risks seem, for unknown reasons, to rise in women who have lupus.

Barrier contraceptives, such as condoms or the diaphragm or cervical cap, are thus the best options. While the statistical track records of these methods are somewhat inferior to that of oral contraceptives, many knowledgeable observers have pointed out that unwanted pregnancies have often been traced to misuse (failing to follow instructions) or disuse (failing to use at all). Condoms, of course, are also the only method of contraception that protects against sexually transmitted diseases including transmission of HIV.

Remember that corticosteroids can cause amenorrhea. If you're taking one of these drugs and you miss a period, don't instantly assume that you're pregnant.

If you are absolutely sure that you don't *ever* want to bear a child—or more children—you can consider the possibility of surgical contraception, the procedure called tubal ligation or "tube tying," which cuts off the route for eggs to find their way to the uterus. While this surgery has been reversed in a few cases, it should be viewed as permanent.

# 10

# The "Other" Lupus: Drugs—and More—That Can Cause Disease

Fred and his wife, Ruth, had been enjoying their new life in Arizona for just about three years when it happened. They're transplanted New Yorkers: Fred is a retired corporate attorney, Ruth a free-lance illustrator of children's books who has continued her career while Fred has concentrated on his great passion, golf—now, a newly leisurely pursuit free of business pressures.

One day, as Fred strolled to the first tee, he suddenly fell to the ground, unconscious. The diagnosis was atrial fibrillation, a form of cardiac arrhythmia, irregular heartbeat. Fred's internist referred him to a cardiologist, who prescribed procainamide, a drug that, taken daily, acts to stabilize the heartbeat. That seemed to solve the problem, and Fred returned to his golf game with confidence and enthusiasm.

A few months went by before it became apparent that something was amiss. The first clue was growing fatigue: "He complained of feeling tired all the time," Ruth recalls. Fred phoned his cardiologist, who seemed unconcerned. "I got no sympathy at all," he declares. "He simply advised me to get more exercise—but I was much too tired to follow that advice."

Then, a week later, Fred fell. It wasn't renewed arrhythmia— his heartbeat remained strong and regular—and he didn't lose consciousness: "One leg just buckled under me, and I thought I'd just developed a trick knee. It happened again, and again. And then a fourth time—but I fell toward the other side; it was the *other* leg that buckled. And I thought, no, not *two* trick knees. It was about time for my annual checkup, so I made an appointment with my internist, and when I went for my exam, I told him about the problem."

Fred's general internist, unlike his cardiologist, was concerned: "He checked me thoroughly, and he found severe muscle weakness in both thighs. The muscles were just wasted. He said he suspected drug-induced lupus. He stopped the procainamide and put me on a different drug for the arrhythmia. He also prescribed a short course of prednisone. And he ordered blood tests, which confirmed the diagnosis."

Fred is now doing fine on the new drug; he's also having physical therapy, at his doctor's suggestion, to regain his muscle strength, and he's put the experience behind him. Ruth looks back on it with more indignation: "Knowing what we know now, the cardiologist should have followed up. He should have responded right away to Fred's complaint of fatigue."

Ruth is right—not only because any physician should respond to a patient's report of a new symptom, but because the possibility of the complication Fred suffered should have come instantly to mind.

## Not Quite the Same

Fred's internist used the most common term for his affliction, *drug-induced lupus*; another is *drug-related lupus*. Since we now know that medications aren't the only substances to induce the condition, and that it also differs in significant ways from the chronic disorder known as lupus, a third term—*lupus-like syndrome (LLS)*—is more accurate.

There are no established criteria for the diagnosis of LLS. Often, there are only one or two symptoms. As in Fred's case, fatigue and weakness are frequently prominent; joint pain is often a significant complaint as well. There may also be fever, a rash, headache, or chest pain. Much less commonly, anemia or kidney involvement may occur—but never central nervous system symptoms, which can occur in "regular" lupus.

Laboratory tests show both similarities and distinct differences. One lab test in LLS induced by medications is always positive: the test for antinuclear antibodies (ANA)—which is positive, you'll recall, in most but not all lupus patients. A test for antibodies to a widely distributed protein called histone is positive in a reported 90 to 100 percent (only 30 to 50 percent of lupus patients will test positive for such antibodies). Fewer than 5 percent of those with LLS develop antibodies to double-stranded or "native" DNA (dsDNA), found in 50 to 60 percent of lupus patients. Nor do they have any of the "special" antibodies to extractable nuclear antigens cited in chapter 2— anti-Sm, anti-Ro, anti-La, and anti-nRNP.

The main, and ultimately completely defining, difference between lupus and LLS is that once the drug or other substance causing LLS is withdrawn, the illness abates (and will return if the stimulus is restored—a confirmation established in research but, of course, not normally done with actual patients).

This doesn't necessarily happen overnight; resolution of the symptoms, as well as any physical impact (Fred's muscle weakness, for example), may take time and even require therapy—a short course of low-dose corticosteroids, as in Fred's case, or analgesics, or physical therapy. But the condition will not progress and is not chronic, assuming the precipitating cause is removed.

## The Medications

Many drugs have been implicated in precipitating a lupus-like syndrome, and the one first prescribed for Fred's cardiac arrhythmia, procainamide (Procan, Pronestyl), leads the list. It triggers the syndrome in up to one-third of those taking it. (The incidence appears to be a bit lower with a recently introduced variant called acetyl procainamide.)

Other drugs on which authorities agree are hydralazine (Apresoline, also a number of brand-named combinations), a drug prescribed to treat hypertension; chlorpromazine (Thorazine), an antipsychotic and anti-nausea agent; certain anticonvulsants; the antituberculosis drug isoniazid; some sulfa drugs; and oral contraceptives (my first directive to a new patient who has lupus-like symptoms and is taking the Pill is to discontinue it). Still other agents have come under suspicion from time to time, including other drugs used in the treatment of high blood pressure.

Such a reaction was first recorded in the 1940s, and the drug was a sulfonamide. Hydralazine was the second therapeutic agent found at fault, in 1953, and procainamide was the third, identified in 1962.

The medication most recently singled out is lovastatin (Mevacor), a cholesterol-lowering drug introduced in 1987.By 1991, it had been added to the list of drugs capable of causing a lupus-like syndrome, with symptoms and laboratory test results similar to those earlier reported with other drugs. Two chemically related drugs for the same purpose, pravastatin (Pravachol) and simvastatin (Zocor), recently completed clinical trials and have become available for prescription. Early reports indicated adverse effects similar to those of lovastatin, including myositis (muscle inflammation); whether they can also cause LLS remains to be seen.

In chapter 3, I noted that there are apparently hereditary factors governing susceptibility to lupus. In the drug-induced syndrome, too, there may be some such factors. In the cases of the two most prominent medications, investigators have found distinct associations with HLA markers—though *not* the same ones singled out in association with lupus itself. I noted in chapter 3 that DR2 and DR3 had been especially linked with lupus. In LLS patients who have reacted to procainamide, the association is with DR6, found in a reported 53 percent (versus 17 percent of control subjects); in those reacting to hydralazine, the association is with DR4, found in 73 percent (vs. 32 percent of controls).

The number of subjects in these studies has been small, and the proof of hereditary susceptibility is not, at this point, overwhelming. This possible genetic connection does nevertheless underscore a previous observation: Some people break down, or metabolize, certain drugs in the body faster than others. Involved in this process is an enzyme, produced by the liver, called acetyltransferase. Individuals who metabolize the drugs in question quickly are known as rapid acetylators, and they have a relatively high level of acetyltransferase activity; those who take longer are called slow acetylators, and they have a lower enzyme activity level. Whether one is a fast or slow acetylator is known to be genetically determined, and the

U.S. population is more or less evenly divided between the two types of people.

Drugs such as procainamide and hydralazine, which happen to require acetylation, can induce LLS in both fast and slow acetylators. But the time required is markedly different. One study, for example, followed a number of patients taking procainamide for cardiac arrhythmias; after six months on the drug, all the slow acetylators had developed antinuclear antibodies (ANA), while only a third of the rapid acetylators had done so. The positive blood test is *not* necessarily predictive of the syndrome—although if LLS does develop, it seems to be more likely to develop in slow acetylators, and it is likely to develop substantially earlier. But the time may still be months, or even a full year.

Two points should be made about the acetylation phenomenon. One is that while procainamide, hydralazine, and certain other drugs linked to LLS require acetylation in the metabolization process, some others also known to trigger LLS do not. Acetyltransferase activity level is therefore not a consistent factor in the occurrence of the drug-induced syndrome.

Second, the phenomenon may or may not have implications for lupus itself. It has *not* been demonstrated that there is a substantially higher proportion of slow acetylators among people with lupus than among the general population, although this question is still under study, and some investigators feel that the proportion is *somewhat* higher. Those who are working with the laboratory mice mentioned earlier—the inbred strains which spontaneously develop a lupus-like illness—are attempting to explore the acetylation question in the animals as well.

## Other LLS-Inducing Agents

In addition to certain medications, other agents have also been linked to remarkably lupus-like syndromes. The reports have been far less frequent, but those that have appeared have been thought-provoking.

Hydralazine is a hydrazine compound, and in at least one reported incident, the chemical has induced a lupus-like syndrome in a laboratory technician who had been exposed to it in her work, simply by its touching her skin. There was complete correlation between remission and removal of the substance from her environment. There was also complete correlation between recurrence and re-exposure to the chemical (done deliberately, with the patient's cooperation, under medically supervised challenge).

Another substance reliably documented in this regard is alfalfa. A researcher testing the cholesterol-lowering potential of alfalfa seeds in monkeys and rabbits met with dire results in his primate subjects, a group of female macaques; three of five animals fed the seeds as supplements to a nourishing diet developed a syndrome that included facial rash, hair loss, hemolytic anemia, and high ANA levels, and one died of infection (the other two survived after a course of corticosteroid treatment).The researcher himself—who had ingested some seeds in order to observe the effect in humans—found that his cholesterol level dropped; he also developed anemia, other blood-cell abnormalities, and antinuclear antibodies.

## Breast Implants

And there is the still-unresolved, and profoundly disturbing, question of silicone gel breast implants. In recent years, some 150,000 American women a year have received implants, 20 percent for reconstruction following cancer surgery and the remainder for cosmetic enhancement.

Although they had been in use since the 1960s, no definitive safety studies had ever been undertaken. The 1976 medical-device law giving the U.S. Food and Drug Administration (FDA) authority over such implants "grandfathered" (gave automatic marketing approval to) devices already in wide use, while reserving to the agency the right to demand answers should questions of safety or effectiveness later arise. It was only in 1988 that the FDA notified manufacturers of the silicone gel implants that evidence of their safety would be required.

Risks of the implants had long been known to include scar tissue and hardening; the possibility of the implant's obstructing cancer-detection imaging; and migration of gel outside an implant's envelope, with unknown impact on other parts of the body. (This last concern did *not* apply to implants in which the outer silicone envelope contains, instead of silicone gel, normal saline—a neutral solution that reflects the body's own chemical balance and is, by definition, completely innocuous.) By early 1991, a possible cancer link was reported—but only to one brand of implant, since withdrawn from the market, in which the silicone envelope was sheathed with a polyurethane foam.

The main concern has focused on reports of autoimmune disease, apparently resulting from the antigenic action of silicone gel, either leaked from intact implants or spilled when the envelopes ruptured. Isolated reports had appeared in the medical literature as early as the 1980s. The syndromes have been variously described as "like" scleroderma (skin thickening, a prominent characteristic of an autoimmune disorder, progressive systemic sclerosis, that may affect various parts of the body); resembling rheumatoid arthritis; or lupus-like. In a few cases, conditions much like Sjögren's syndrome have been seen, albeit without the usual antibodies—anti-Ro, anti-La—usually associated with Sjögren's.

Several series of women with silicone gel implants and symptoms suggesting connective-tissue disease were described at a 1992 American College of Rheumatology meeting, by physicians from various parts of the country.

Fifty such women, for example, were seen through 1991 at the University of South Florida College of Medicine rheumatology clinic. They had received their implants an average of four and a half years before symptoms developed, and the average age of the group was forty-three. The women's symptoms included fatigue (84 percent), joint pain (60 percent), Raynaud's phenomenon (14 percent), and others. Tests for ANA were positive in 38 percent. At the time the clinicians reported their data, thirty-three of the fifty patients had elected to have the implants removed. (If the implants have leaked, and silicone has migrated to other parts of the body, removal of the implants may not necessarily end the symptoms.)

Another fifty women, seen over an eighteen-month period, were described at the ACR meeting by physicians from UCLA. Their patients' average age was forty-five, and their implants had been in place, on average, just under seven years. All the women in this series had suffered joint pain, chiefly in shoulders, fingers, and knees; among other symptoms noted were fatigue (78 percent), Sjögren's-like dryness of eyes or mouth (60 percent), and Raynaud's (48 percent). ANA tests were positive in 70 percent.

Not surprisingly, reassurances had been issued by the makers of the products. A 1991 statement distributed by the then leading implant manufacturer, Dow Corning (a joint operation of the two corporations), explained that the concerns about autoimmune disorders were "only hypothetical questions"—although its package inserts, intended for physicians, acknowledged "reports of suspected immunological responses" and stated that, "Many of the case reports suggest systemic illness with joint pain, myositis [muscle inflammation], fever, and lymphadenopathy [enlarged lymph nodes] being most frequently mentioned."

The inserts went on to list "additional symptoms claimed," including "chronic arthropathy [joint disease], morphea [isolated spots of skin thickening], keratoconjunctivitis sicca [eye inflammation with deficiency of tears, one form of Sjögren's syndrome], pyrexia [fever], skin lesions, arthralgia [joint pain], and alopecia [hair loss]." (I have no idea why some symptoms were listed twice.)

In a separate piece of lay literature, offering "supplemental information," Dow addressed the subject with the confusing declaration that, "It cannot be said with assurance whether silicone breast implants are associated with diseases of the immune system, or whether abnormalities in the immune system cause connective tissue disease."

Some of the statements that followed that one were similarly disquieting: A circulatory problem referred to as "Raynard's" (presumably Raynaud's) syndrome was mentioned. A definition of connective tissue listed "bone" as an example. Lupus was twice characterized as "rare." A catalog of sites that might be affected in lupus included the skin, joints, blood vessels, and "membranes that surround the lungs and heart" but omitted the kidneys, mucous membranes, blood cells, and the lungs and heart themselves.

Dow Corning was one of seven firms supplying silicone gel implants. Only two remain in the business at this writing.

By January 1992, the FDA had concluded that there were sufficient data to call the safety of the silicone implants into question, and the agency asked physicians to stop inserting them and manufacturers to stop supplying them, pending review by a special panel of additional data, including material from manufacturers' files as well as physicians' reports.

The following month, the panel of experts announced its finding that, while the link with autoimmune disease was still inconclusive, the data failed to demonstrate the implants' safety. Rates of rupture and leakage, as well as the frequency of autoimmune disease to which silicone might be linked, could not be established. The panel recommended that use of the silicone implants be restricted to patients admitted to clinical study projects, with the goal of answering those safety questions. All those wishing reconstruction following cancer surgery would be eligible, as would those with serious breast deformities, but availability of the silicone implants for cosmetic purposes would likely be sharply curtailed. In April 1992, the FDA issued an order implementing the panel's recommendations.

The following September, the FDA announced strict study protocols. Under them, women (at least eighteen years old) can receive the implants only (1) after mastectomy or other breast cancer treatment (this includes women who have had unsuccessful attempts at reconstruction with saline implants or self-tissue grafting); (2) because of severe deformity, as certified by a physician; or (3) because previously implanted silicone gel implants need to be replaced for medical reasons. In short, there is no provision for use of these implants for purely cosmetic purposes.

Further, the protocols explicitly exclude women who have lupus or scleroderma; are pregnant or breast-feeding; have an abscess or infection anywhere in the body; have any disease or condition, including uncontrolled diabetes, that could affect healing; have "incompatible tissue characteristics" (such as radiation damage, or a compromised blood supply to the area); pose any unwarranted surgical risks.

Physicians who implant the silicone gel implants are responsible for making sure patients meet all the criteria and can't use saline implants instead; they must also use an officially approved patient consent form. The physician is also required to keep comprehensive patient records; notify the manufacturer of each procedure and supply data for the patient registry; and provide the patient with full information on her implant, including brand name and model number.

A toll-free consumer-information line on this subject, (800) 532-4440, is maintained by the FDA. A recording gives the latest news on the status of breast implants, and callers can leave their names and addresses to receive a package of updated printed materials.

The manufacturer maintaining the clinical studies monitor is the Mentor Corporation of Santa Barbara, California. Physicians can obtain a list of participating researchers, as well as additional information, by calling Mentor's toll-free number, (800) 525-6747.

The most recent studies announced at this writing have confirmed the wisdom of these warnings and precautions. University of California, Davis, researchers told the spring 1993 meeting of the American Academy of Allergy and Immunology that evaluation of more than 100 women with silicone breast implants showed 35 percent had developed autoantibodies—specifically, antibodies against the connective-tissue component collagen. Two recent animal studies conducted in laboratory rats, one by Dow Corning (which, as noted, no longer makes the implants), resulted in what the FDA characterized as "a strong antibody response."

Saline breast implants remain available, but in January 1993, the FDA proposed that their makers also be required to demonstrate the safety of those devices. Thus far, there have been no large-scale reports of any of the sort of complications seen or suspected with the silicone products.

## If You Have Silicone Gel Implants

Probably only in a minority of cases, among those thousands of women who have had the implants, have complications occurred. Ruptured or leaking implants should be removed. While ruptures may be detectable by mammography (breast X ray), it should not be used for that purpose in the absence of symptoms, since it exposes healthy breast tissue to unnecessary radiation. Leaks and ruptures can often be discerned by experienced radiologists using other techniques, including ultrasound and magnetic resonance imaging (MRI).

As previously noted, no one really knows how often leaks or ruptures occur. Estimates of rupture rates alone have ranged from less than 1 percent according to manufacturers to as high as 25 percent and more in some reports from physicians; the FDA's estimate, at this writing, is 4 to 6 percent.

There is no need or reason to remove silicone gel implants that have caused no problems and have not leaked or ruptured, but the FDA advises that women who have such implants should take several precautions:

- Have regular breast examinations by your physician.

- Be familiar with the appearance and feeling of your breasts and see your physician immediately if you observe or experience any change.

- Promptly report any unusual symptoms to your physician,

whether or not you believe they may be related to your breast implants.

- Have mammography for the detection of breast cancer at the intervals recommended for women in your age group. (If you have had breast-cancer surgery, consult your physician about the necessity for mammography.)

- Realize that implants can interfere with mammography by casting a "shadow" on the X-ray "picture" and any scarring can also distort the image; they also prevent the breast's being compressed to the degree necessary to obtain the best quality mammogram. This is of serious concern, since statistics show that survival rates are dramatically higher for women who have the very small breast cancers only mammography can detect, as opposed to those that have grown large enough to be obvious to the touch.

  To counter those drawbacks, special techniques are needed. Be sure your mammography facility has personnel trained and experienced in these techniques. You can call the National Cancer Institute information service toll-free, (800) 4-CANCER [(800) 422-6237], to get the names of facilities in your area accredited by the American College of Radiology; such facilities are more likely than others to offer the necessary expertise. Double-check when you make an appointment—and when you have a mammogram, be sure to tell both the technician and the radiologist that you have implants.

- Women with silicone gel implants may also want to consider exchanging them for saline implants. Author Betty Rollin (*First, You Cry*), who had two of the latter inserted a number of years ago following her second mastectomy, observed in a *New York Times* essay published in early 1992 at the height of the public controversy that, "Cosmetically, saline has gotten a bad rap." While admitting that the saline devices may sometimes harden or, conversely, dramatically deflate if a leak develops, she pointed out that such problems are easily repaired using local anesthesia—and, "If saline leaks, it's only water."

# CHAPTER
# 11

# Food Boosts, Cosmetic Cautions, and Other Practical Pointers

Chapter 10 singled out certain medications and other agents known or suspected to cause not lupus per se, but a lupus-like syndrome (LLS)—a condition that ceases once the trigger substance has been withdrawn or removed. No one has suggested that these substances cause lupus itself. Yet it seems to me, and to many other observers, that if you already *have* lupus, it doesn't make sense to expose yourself to such potential troublemakers unnecessarily, since they may make your disease worse.

One of the LLS precipitators noted in chapter 10, in fact, has been known to do just that. Several years ago, physicians reported two cases of lupus patients who had severe flares after they'd enjoyed long remissions on low doses of prednisone. In both cases, the flares followed the patients' consumption of alfalfa tablets purchased at a health-food store.

The two leading drugs known to induce a lupus-like syndrome—procainamide and hydralazine—involve chemicals known as hydrazines and amines, which also occur in many other products. (A related chemical is present, as it happens, in alfalfa seeds and sprouts.) Encounters with some of these can't be escaped. Some, on the other hand, are easily avoided.

Hydrazine and its derivatives are found, among other places, in herbicides, pesticides, photographic supplies, and dyes—as well as in mushrooms (in which hydrazine occurs naturally). A chemical cousin of hydrazine, called tartrazine, is found in the form of a coloring known technically as FD&C Yellow No. 5, used in many cosmetics and food products ranging from hair rinses and bath salts to prepared breakfast cereals and some soft drinks. (The letters in front of the color stand for "food, drug, and cosmetic" and signify that the coloring may be used in all three classes of products.)

Aromatic amines also occur as breakdown products of some food dyes, as well as in permanent hair colorings. Both hydrazines and amines are constituents of tobacco smoke—which, it has now been confirmed, poses almost as much of a danger to the secondhand, or "passive," recipient of the smoke as it does to the smoker.

How about silicone gel breast implants, which I discussed at some length in the previous chapter?

The American College of Rheumatology's cautious official position on the subject: "It seems advisable that patients with rheumatic disease not undergo elective augmentation mammoplasty with silicone." As I noted in chapter 10, the FDA has in fact gone further: The protocols for the safety studies that are now under way on these products specifically exclude lupus patients from participation.

If silicone gel implants are at some point again permitted to be marketed unrestrictedly, I would still advise lupus patients—and others as well—to avoid the silicone gel implants. If you feel that breast-enlargement or reconstruction surgery is necessary, insist on saline implants.

## What You Eat

After her lupus was diagnosed, Elizabeth determined to do everything possible to take care of her health, and she knew that meant eating right: "I went to a nutritionist. I thought I knew everything, but I found I knew absolutely nothing. She asked me to describe what I ate, and I mentioned something about ordering a hamburger and throwing away the bun. She said, 'It would be better to eat the bun and throw away the hamburger!' I do try to eat as little fat as possible, just as a general rule, although I know it doesn't do anything special for lupus. Actually, I haven't really found that any food, or the absence of it, has any significance for lupus."

Jan has mixed feelings about the role that what she eats might play. She notes that her sister Shirley, who is a faithful vegetarian, also has lupus, but, in contrast to Jan's multiple-drug regimen, has done well on piroxicam (Feldene), a nonsteroidal anti-inflammatory agent (NSAID), alone: "I said to her, 'I wonder why your disease is so mild.' She said, 'It's my lifestyle. It's because I'm a vegetarian, and I take vitamins.' Okay, I tried it. And for a while, I did feel better. Then, about six weeks into it, I got a flare—so it obviously didn't work all that well. On the other hand, it does seem to me I feel worse after eating red meat—which happens to be my favorite thing in the whole world."

No one has carried out controlled scientific studies of any size examining the effects of diet on lupus. Doing so would be difficult, given the come-and-go nature of the disease and the subtle, long-term impact of our eating habits on our health and our lives.

Experiments with the mouse models that have provided so many helpful clues to human lupus do tell us something, however. A number of such studies have demonstrated that changing the animals' diet balance, raising the percentage of complex carbohydrates and sharply cutting the proportion of protein, protected the mice from glomerulonephritis and prolonged their lives. Curtailment of total calories, even without changing the balance, provided similar benefits.

Physicians in all specialties, especially cardiologists and kidney experts, agree that Americans in general eat a great deal more meat—and animal proteins in general—than they need or is good for them. Despite Jan's flare (which may have stemmed from something else in her life), her sister may have a point. Antigens—the trouble triggers in lupus—are, after all, proteins, whether foreign or self. Fewer animal proteins may mean less trouble.

I don't suggest you necessarily drum all animal protein out of your diet, but you might consider an ovolactovegetarian diet (which permits eggs and dairy products)—or just eating a little less meat and a little more of the other food groups: grains, cereals, fruits and vegetables, and so on. It certainly won't hurt you.

Concerned health professionals are also in agreement that Americans in general consume considerably larger quantities of saturated fats and salt than is necessary or desirable. In fact, if you never use butter or cream or add salt to food, and you shun all animal fat, you will not suffer at all nutritionally. Many people who have abandoned salt, both at the table and in the kitchen, and instead make use of an array of herbs and spices, find they are now enjoying a much more tasty menu.[*]

In the interest of avoiding alien chemicals as much as possible, I also suggest placing emphasis on fresh foods rather than prepared-food products, which contain all sorts of preservatives and other additives, as well as more salt than anyone should consume. And certainly foods known to contain hydrazines and amines—mushrooms, alfalfa seeds and sprouts and most other legumes, possibly some smoked foods—should be avoided.

While some have counseled against the addition to the diet of vitamin and mineral supplements, my feeling is that not only are the "recommended daily allowances" of most supplements lower than conducive to optimum health, but most people don't receive even those quantities of these essential nutrients from their diets. In my own practice, I do recommend supplementation, consisting of at least a single daily tablet containing standard quantities of the major vitamins and minerals—i.e., that minimal "daily allowance."

An important recent realization is that some of these elements—notably, vitamins C and E and beta carotene (an important substance in the formation of vitamin A, found in carrots as well as in other orange and yellow vegetables)—act as *anti-oxidants*. Oxidation now appears to be the chemical process that turns cholesterol into a lethal clogger of arteries.

---

[*]In the matter of dietary fats, one highly informative guide is Kathleen Mayes's *Fighting Fat* (Pennant Books, 1989), which sounds like a weight-loss manual but isn't (although shedding excess pounds may be one result of heeding Mayes's advice).

While this process is a threat to us all, persons with lupus are especially likely to display high lipid levels (lipids include cholesterol as well as other undesirable substances such as triglycerides). Steroid treatment may increase the hazard.

As you may know, both total cholesterol levels and comparative levels of two subtypes are important in predicting heart-disease risk, and these subtypes have emerged as perhaps even more significant. The two are HDL (high-density lipoprotein) cholesterol, a higher ratio of which appears to be protective, and the L(low)DL—or, worse, V(very)LDL—type, a higher level of which raises the risk of heart disease.

A study reported at the 1992 international conference on lupus, held in London, found that these risk factors were consistently increased in lupus patients generally, and especially in those on prednisone. A New York University Medical Center analysis reported in late 1992 underscored these findings; it was clear that lupus patients had higher levels of cholesterol generally, as well as lower levels of HDLs and higher levels of triglycerides.

Thus, it appears sensible for lupus patients—and particularly those taking steroids—to pay careful attention to diet advice that will diminish a rise in lipids.

If you're sensitive to light, also see the note on foods in the following section.

## Sun and Other Light

At least a third of people with lupus are photosensitive; sunlight, and some other light as well, can trigger not only skin reactions but even full-fledged flares of the disease. How ultraviolet light sets off this process is not well understood, but the fact that it can do so is well documented. By and large, lighter-skinned people are more apt to be photosensitive, but that isn't completely, dependably consistent.

Lisa is photosensitive, and this has led to a job change: "Landscaping turned out to be the worst occupation I could have chosen, having to be outdoors all the time. I should have stopped when I was diagnosed, but I continued. Two years ago, I finally decided to switch, and I was really lucky: I found a terrific job with an interior design firm, working with plants. It's sort of indoor landscaping, and it's been fun."

She hasn't shunned the sun completely, though. "In the summer," she says, "I usually get a pretty bad rash on my face and neck and arms—in *spite* of the sunscreen, and the hat, and the long sleeves." But she goes on to admit that, "My husband and I have a boat, and I do go out on the boat—although I try to stay under cover as much as possible. I also like to garden, but I try to do it after 4 P.M. Sometimes I guess I push it a little."

Lisa's reaction has been limited to a rash, and she's willing to risk that, to some extent, for favorite recreations. That's her choice. Lupus patients who are photosensitive and have systemic reactions, which could threaten organ damage, are taking a far more serious risk if they don't take stringent precautions against exposure.

That doesn't mean you need to go to the extreme of staying indoors with the shades drawn on sunny days. (Actually, clouds don't offer any substantial protection; they block visible light to a far greater extent than the damaging ultraviolet.) But broad-brimmed hats and long sleeves are helpful. And the use of a sunscreen—with an SPF (sun protection factor) as high as possible—is a must; the product should promise protection against both kinds of ultraviolet light, UVA and UVB. If you have a history of allergies, as many people with lupus do, you may want to look for a brand that doesn't contain para-aminobenzoic acid (PABA) or padimate, fairly common ingredients to which some people are sensitive.

Be aware, too, that reflected light can be just as damaging as direct light; light is especially strongly reflected from sand, water, or snow. I flatly advise photosensitive patients to shun beaches and boats, as well as golf courses, ski slopes, and other unshaded outdoor areas—summer *or* winter. And tanning salons, despite safety claims they may make, are off limits as well. You should also avoid exposure to unshielded fluorescent bulbs, since those bulbs emit substantial amounts of ultraviolet light.

And ultraviolet emissions may also involve ordinary office copiers. One case reported at the American College of Rheumatology's 1992 meeting highlighted a lupus patient who had had repeated occupational exposure to copier flash lamps, with exacerbation of skin problems. (She was often required to copy from books and journals, with the copier cover open.) Experimental testing reproduced the symptoms; a change in the occupational environment cured the problem and the patient's complications.

Finally, you should know that certain foods and drugs can increase photosensitivity. The foods that can do this are all plants containing chemicals called *psoralens*, which act, in the body, to enhance the effects of the sun; prominent among them are lemons, limes, celery, parsnips, parsley, and figs. Some people who *don't* have lupus have even been known to suffer painful and unsightly skin eruptions when they've spilled lemonade on their skin on a bright, sunny day. (This chemical reaction is actually used beneficially in the therapy for psoriasis called PUVA, an acronym for "psoralen plus ultraviolet A," which has proved effective for that skin condition.)

Among the drugs that can heighten photosensitivity are some of the tetracyclines; piroxicam (Feldene), the anti-inflammatory agent Jan's sister Shirley takes (obviously, she isn't sun-sensitive, or her physician would not have prescribed it); hydrochlorothiazide, a diuretic and anti-hypertension drug (Esidrix, HydroDiuril, Oretic); as well as some sulfa drugs, antiseizure medications, and antidepressants. Be sure to mention photosensitivity to any doctor who's prescribing a medication of any kind for you; there is almost always an alternative.

## The Cosmetic Counter

The skin is quite a miraculous organ. Partly, it's protective, shielding our insides from a frequently hostile environment. But substances can enter the body through the skin as well. Indeed, pharmaceutical designers have in some instances deliberately used the skin as a portal for drug delivery. Among chemicals that have been administered to the inside of the body via patches placed on the outside are estrogens; agents to allay motion sickness; relievers of chest pain in heart-disease patients; and, most recently, nicotine to help smokers break the habit of inhaling the drug.

As I've said, I think it's not smart to expose our bodies to unnecessary chemicals—and I firmly believe cosmetics are in that category. They contain many ingredients, not all of them tested; among those ingredients are a host of dyes, including tartrazine, a form of hydrazine. Nail lacquers contain sulfonamide, one of the agents noted in chapter 10 to be implicated in causing a lupus-like syndrome. A range of cosmetic preparations, including permanent hair colorings, can set off allergic reactions, to which people with lupus are often especially susceptible.

I must admit that I haven't been successful in persuading a great number of my patients to abandon cosmetics altogether. If you feel, as many women do, that appearing in public with no makeup at all is unthinkable, I urge that you at least use makeup very, very lightly and that you switch to one of the hypoallergenic brands from which substances most likely to act as allergens have been excluded. And please avoid permanent hair colorings, which contain agents from the family of amines and have been definitely implicated in the activation of lupus. (Simple hair *lighteners* are safe.)

## A Dental-Care Precaution

A significant minority of lupus patients have a condition called Libman-Sacks endocarditis (after the doctors who first described it), or verrucous endocarditis, in which tiny, wart-like growths develop on the valves between chambers of the heart (*verruca* is Latin for "wart").

This condition may be suspected if the physician detects a heart sound called an *organic murmur* (there are many, many kinds of heart murmurs), which signals some structural change. The presence of the valve lesions can then be detected by echocardiography, a technique that employs sound waves to create a visual image of the interior of the heart. In most cases, the lesions cause no serious problems unless they become infected.

The majority of those with the lesions appear to test positive for anti-cardiolipin (ACL) antibody (see chapter 9), as well as for antibody to nRNP, one of the nuclear proteins I mentioned in chapter 2.

An infection of Libman-Sacks lesions, known as subacute bacterial endocarditis, can occur as a result of dental treatment, when bacteria—prominently, streptococci—may easily slip into the bloodstream and find their way to the heart. If you have Libman-Sacks lesions, it's wise to take prophylactic antibiotics before and after any dental procedure that could possibly involve any bleeding whatever; for most people, that includes routine checkups.

The antibiotic—usually amoxicillin, or another member of the penicillin family, or erythromycin in cases of penicillin allergy—is taken an hour or two before, and again a few hours after, the dental treatment, the exact times depending on the drug. Preferably, put your dentist and your rheumatologist in touch with each other, so they can discuss the best preventive strategy for you.

Dental procedures are of particular concern because the mouth happens to be a hotbed of bacteria, and most people visit their dentists fairly regularly. Other, less frequent procedures that could conceivably cause a break in mucous membrane and send bacteria into the bloodstream call for similar precautions; they include gynecological procedures such as Pap smears, as well as gastrointestinal probes such as sigmoidoscopy or colonoscopy.

Infection of Libman-Sacks lesions, should it occur, is a medical emergency and is life-threatening unless promptly treated. (Symptoms consist mainly of initial fever followed by signs of heart failure, including irregular heartbeat and difficulty in breathing.)

If you have Sjögren's syndrome, you need to be concerned about another aspect of dental care. See the following section.

## Notes on Sjögren's Syndrome

About 5 percent of those with lupus also suffer from Sjögren's syndrome, a condition of extreme dryness in certain areas due to dysfunction of various moisture-producing glands, prominently the salivary and lacrimal (tear) glands; it's sometimes called "sicca syndrome," from the Latin for "dry."* The syndrome also occurs in people who do not have lupus. In those who have Sjögren's alone, often then called "primary" Sjögren's, more than 60 percent have anti-La antibodies and over 90 percent have anti-Ro (see chapter 2), but in lupus patients who also have Sjögren's, the proportions are somewhat lower.

If the eyes are affected, there is usually a sensation of "something in the eye"; some describe the sensation as "burning" or "gritty." There may also be redness and itching and other discomfort. A decrease in saliva leads to extreme dryness of the mouth, with difficulty in chewing and swallowing, constant thirst, and possibly soreness and cracking in and around the mouth and lips.

There are a number of products available for relief, including "artificial tears" and "artificial saliva" sprays; sugarless lozenges are often suggested, too, for mouth dryness. Too-low humidity can further irritate dry eyes, so a humidifier may help.

Most of the artificial-tears products—which must be used regularly, not just when there's marked discomfort—contain preservatives to which some people are allergic, with the result that the condition isn't relieved but aggravated. A few products without preservatives are also available.

If you have mouth dryness, medically termed *xerostomia*, you need to take steps to prevent serious dental problems, since one function of saliva is to help wash away plaque, the invisible bacterial film that forms constantly on the teeth and

---

*The condition was first described in the 1930s by Henrik Sjögren, a Swedish ophthalmologist; he noted that his patients' eye dryness seemed to be associated with xerostomia—dry mouth—as well.

precipitates cavities and periodontal disease.

Regular dental visits are very important, as is scrupulous at-home tooth care, including plaque control (use a soft-bristled toothbrush and an anti-plaque fluoride toothpaste and rinse, and floss daily). Avoid candy and other sugar-heavy foods and soft drinks; stick to sugar-free chewing gum. You might also talk to your dentist about topical fluoride applications that will help provide further resistance to cavities.

Sometimes, mouth and/or eye dryness is accompanied by uncomfortable nasal dryness as well. Again, there's a nonprescription solution: Try one of the several brands of saline nasal mists that come in spray bottles. *Don't* confuse these products—which are also effective for the nasal stuffiness accompanying a cold—with decongestant sprays; the salines are not medicated, can be used as often as desired, and will not cause the "rebound" stuffiness often seen with the decongestants.

In a few women, Sjögren's may affect the lubricating glands of the vagina, making sexual intercourse extremely painful. The solution is to use a lubricant; I recommend a water-soluble type such as KY jelly, since such oil-based products as petroleum jelly can be absorbed and are capable of causing circulatory complications. Oil-based products can also degrade the latex in condoms, diaphragms, and cervical caps, rendering those barrier methods of contraception ineffective.

## How About Shots?

Lupus patients may be particularly susceptible to infection—especially if they are taking corticosteroids or immunosuppressants—and should protect themselves as much as possible. Sensible precautions include taking care of one's general health and, if possible, staying out of sneezing, coughing crowds. What about immunizations, routine and other?

The question has been somewhat controversial. There is general agreement that lupus patients, like other adults, should receive a diphtheria-tetanus shot every ten years, and that the vaccines against influenza and pneumococcal pneumonia are helpful (concerns that these vaccines might trigger flares have not been borne out in studies). Flu shots are needed annually, since the viruses mutate frequently, and the vaccine is reformulated each year to incorporate newly identified strains.

There have been some reports of a lower level of response to these vaccines in lupus patients, and your physician may want to do blood tests to be sure the level of protection is adequate; the pneumonia vaccine may also have to be given more often, because the level of protection may fall unusually quickly.

If for some reason you did not have the standard childhood immunizations—they include, in addition to diphtheria and tetanus, pertussis (whooping cough), measles, mumps, rubella, *Haemophilus influenzae* type B, and hepatitis B—discuss with your physician the advisability of having them now. Some are more important than others. Pertussis, for instance, is a less severe illness with increased age, while rubella poses a particularly serious peril if it's contracted in pregnancy.

As to *non*-routine immunizations—that is, vaccination for travel—very few countries still require vaccination as a condition for entry. For most diseases endemic to specific areas, vaccines are not generally considered necessary unless the traveler will be going into rural areas, areas far from cities, airports, and so on, which are probably best avoided. The wisest course would be not to plan trips to areas in which serious infectious diseases are either endemic or epidemic.

Current information on specific destinations, including disease risks and recommended protective measures, is available via the Centers for Disease Control and Prevention's interactive International Traveler's Hotline, (404) 332-4559; the call must be placed from a touch-tone telephone. The CDC also publishes a periodically revised book, *Health Information for International Travel*; for information on the latest edition, contact the Superintendent of Documents, U.S. Government Printing Office, Washington DC 20402, (202) 783-3238.

One other, usually "childhood," disease must be mentioned. As this is written, there is not yet a generally available vaccine for chickenpox (although one is under consideration by the Food and Drug Administration). If you have never had chickenpox, and a vaccine has become available, you should be immunized. If no vaccine has yet been approved, see the special precautionary advice concerning children and teens in chapter 13; it applies to you as well.

## Sexual Activity

The subject of sex is one that comes up in physicians' offices far less often than it should, resulting in a great lack of information that can lead to serious misunderstandings. Both certain medications and lupus itself can have distinct physical impact on sexual activities, impact of which patients—and their partners—should be aware.

Tranquilizers, which are sometimes prescribed to allay anxiety, can occasionally suppress orgasm. Knowledge of this fact can relieve "What did I do wrong?" worries. A man taking medication for hypertension may experience erectile dysfunction ("impotence")—though *not* orgasmic dysfunction (the two are controlled by different nerves); if a change to a drug without this unfortunate side effect is not possible, partners may find gratification by means other than the traditional. Remember that stimulation, for both sexes, can be provided through manual, oral, or other means.

Corticosteroids may cause a number of sexually relevant difficulties. One is decreased libido, or sexual desire (it's *not* personal rejection of the partner), and a little more effort may be required for arousal. Another is easy skin bruisability, suggesting the necessity of a gentler, kinder touch. A third may be osteonecrosis, usually involving a hip joint, which can be quite painful and can interfere with achieving a comfortable position for sexual intercourse (for a full discussion of osteonecrosis, see page 95).

Many lupus patients suffer from mouth ulcers from time to time, which may make once-pleasurable oral sensations associated with sex quite painful. Steroid mouthwashes prescribed by your physician can provide some relief. Similar ulcers may sometimes occur in the vagina; about one in twenty patients experience them. They do go away; until they do, other routes to sexual pleasure might be explored. As I mentioned earlier, vaginal dryness may be a problem in Sjögren's syndrome, and that is easily remedied (see page 177).

Raynaud's phenomenon afflicts some 40 percent of lupus patients, causing pain in the fingers (or toes)—generally in response to cold, but sometimes in reaction to sexual activity as well, because blood flow is diverted to the genital area. A warm room and a warm bath prior to sexual activity can be helpful—and don't lean on your hands during intercourse.

Almost all those with lupus have some joint pain at one time or another. Nonsteroidal anti-inflammatory drugs (NSAIDs) or other pain relievers prescribed or recommended by your doctor may help—and again, a warm bath preceding sex may be useful. Beyond that, some experimentation may be needed to find positioning that minimizes discomfort.

If there's knee pain, for example, avoid flexion, and don't put any weight on the knees; if both knees are involved, avoid intertwining the legs, which will cause increased pain. If one hip, knee, or shoulder is affected, try lying on the side with that joint upward. All-over achiness might suggest achieving sexual gratification by oral or manual activity alone.

When pain, or potential pain, is a chronic presence, it brings with it two other inhibiting factors: There is fear of pain on the part of the patient. And, less often expressed, there is fear of *causing* pain on the part of the patient's partner. Sometimes simple reassurance, in response to that concern, can be extremely helpful. An open mind on the part of both patient and partner, with equally open discussion about both desires and discomforts, is the most valuable aid to satisfying sexual activity.

## The Menopause Question

"I'm looking forward to menopause," declares Jan, who's in her early forties. "My mother had menopause early, so I'm hoping maybe that will happen to me, because I've heard that sometimes, lupus becomes milder then."

That *is* sometimes true, in my observation. There's no guarantee, though, and no one, to my knowledge, has done an extensive survey on the question. Most women, at any rate, don't look forward to menopause, since it can sometimes (*not* always, by any means) be accompanied by uncomfortable symptoms as the body adjusts to a new hormonal pattern.

From a medical viewpoint, the main concern is the increased risk of osteoporosis after menopause. Bone mass peaks in the mid-thirties and gradually declines, at a rate of less than 1 percent per year, after that; the decline accelerates markedly following menopause. The result of this loss of bone mass is susceptibility to fracture, particularly of weight-bearing and much-used joints, the hip in particular. Osteoporosis can also pose a hazard for patients taking corticosteroids, who include virtually all lupus patients at one time or another. There are a number of effective approaches to minimizing the risk of osteoporosis, and I've discussed the problem in detail in chapter 8.

As to the postmenopausal risk of osteoporosis, one proven preventive is hormone replacement therapy—replacement of the estrogens that cease to be produced at menopause. (The estrogen is often coupled with another hormone, progesterone, to minimize the small but real risk of endometrial cancer—cancer of the tissue lining the uterus—that may occur with estrogen alone.) Is this therapy advisable, and safe, in women with lupus?

Opinions differ. Theoretically, estrogens have the potential to worsen lupus; remember that the predominance of lupus is precisely during the childbearing (estrogen-producing) years. On that basis, many rheumatologists would categorically advise against replacement therapy in all lupus patients. I have found that, indeed, when lupus is already severe, estrogen therapy can cause it to worsen.

On the other hand, in mild lupus, the benefits may often outweigh the risks. This is especially true if the patient is a thin, blond person who experienced amenorrhea as a young woman or had low calcium intake as a youngster— i.e., if she has other characteristics predisposing to osteoporosis.

In short, I believe that, as with many other questions, the decision should be made on an individual basis, with informed discussion between physician and patient.

One precaution. Two Australian neurologists were confronted with an aerobics buff—she'd been pursuing the activity for years—who had recently begun suffering severe headaches, lasting several hours, following her exercise classes. She feared a brain tumor or other dire condition, but tests showed nothing of the sort. Questioning revealed that the patient had recently switched from oral to transdermal estrogen replacement—that is, via a skin patch. Intense exercise, the physicians concluded, led to vasodilation, which increased through-the-skin estrogen absorption, raising the blood level suddenly, which in turn precipitated a headache. The doctors' advice: Don't wear the patch during exercise classes.

For the sake of completeness—the data are, at this writing, very preliminary—I should add that an entirely different type of drug is also being explored for the prevention of osteoporosis. That drug is tamoxifen (Nolvadex), an anti-estrogen agent which is used in the treatment of breast cancer (certain breast tumors are encouraged by estrogen). Strangely, there is some evidence that tamoxifen may actually have an effect similar to that of estrogen on the maintenance of bone density and prevention of osteoporosis.

# 12

# The *Rest* of Your Life

If there is a single word that symbolizes lupus for nine out of ten patients, that word is *fatigue*. In fact, asked to describe it, many find themselves at a *loss* for words:

"The fatigue," says Connie, "is just awful. You feel like a wet dishrag, completely helpless and powerless. You can't get rid of that feeling by just lying down for half an hour. I get normally tired, like other people—but this, this is a different kind of tired."

"The worst part," Elizabeth agrees, "is the fatigue. My doctor calls it 'terminal fatigue.' It's a very, very sick feeling, totally overwhelming. I can stand joint pain, but the fatigue is awful. How can I put it? There's just no starch in the body."

"People with lupus," declares Eileen, "need a new word for fatigue, because it's not just simple fatigue as normal people understand it. It's as if you had been forced to stay up—on your feet—for three days straight."

It is, as Connie says, a "different kind of tired." Like Elizabeth's doctor, I have a special phrase for the kind of tiredness my lupus patients experience. I call it "wipe-out fatigue," because it seems to obliterate every ounce of strength, both physical and mental. This fatigue is a very real symptom of lupus and, like other symptoms, deserves treatment—a concept that can be difficult for many people, including people with lupus, to grasp. The treatment is *rest*, in whatever dosage is right for that individual. I tell patients that they *must* rest—and it's just as important as any medication. I say, "Treat this like a prescription."

## Lifestyle Changes

The "different kind of tired" often means a different kind of rest is needed, along with other lifestyle adjustments.

Eileen, an avid traveler, finds that fatigue often strikes when she arrives at her destination: "I've learned that I simply must allow time for the equivalent of a good night's sleep on landing, whatever time of day it is, because only then will I be okay and be able to enjoy the rest of the trip. By that, I don't mean six or eight hours; I mean at least nine or ten hours. If you're a lupus patient, you have to learn to sleep when you need it— even in the middle of the afternoon, if necessary."

That's precisely when Elizabeth has found she needs to rest. An advertising copywriter, she used to report daily to a major Chicago agency. Not long ago, they agreed that, with phones, computers, and fax machines providing instant communication, she could as easily work from home.

The arrangement proved agreeable for employer and employee alike, Elizabeth found: "Except if I'm having a flare, I feel fine in the mornings, so I take advantage of that. I start my working day about 7:30, and I'm great until noontime. I 'meet' my husband for lunch, which he makes; he's retired, so he's home. Then, I go into my 'coma.' That's what I call it. It's a deep, deep sleep; I'm totally out, for two or three hours. It's an absolute necessity."

"Every now and then," she adds, "I decide I must have a day in bed. Maybe I'll decide the evening before, maybe that morning. When it's necessary, it's necessary. You have to let yourself accept that. But the acceptance isn't easy."

It's been especially hard for Jan: "Let's face it, I'm basically a workaholic. It took a while, but I finally realized I can't work the hours I used to, and I let myself get into a more leisurely routine. I get up and, instead of going right to my desk with a mug of coffee the way I used to, I take my pills, and then I go back to bed for forty-five minutes or an hour with the morning paper. Then, I get up and go to work. Often, especially if I'm having a flare, I take afternoon naps."

"And I've realized," she continues, "that my mental energy can flag, too. Sometimes, I can't concentrate at all, and I've found there's no point in going on, so I just stop and watch TV for a while. I've also had to come to terms with feeling guilty because I'm contributing less than I did to our family finances. This is all in my own head, of course; my husband, Charlie, has been totally understanding. And our income hasn't dropped radically. Still, I can't help feeling I'm not doing my share."

Nancy, who was married but is now, as she puts it, "happily divorced" and leading an active social life, sees adequate rest as a vital preventive measure: "My job is highly competitive and demanding. I can't take chances; it just doesn't make sense. I make sure I'm taking care of myself in terms of getting enough sleep. I have a cut-off time; I don't stay out late."

Recognition of the need for rest demands understanding

from others as well: "Usually," says Connie, "I'm a very driven person. I just don't stop. Last year, I was going through a period where I had to have a lot of rest, and I had to cut down on my activity. Mentally, it was very depressing. I'd come home and I couldn't even make dinner. But my family has been pretty wonderful. My husband's an extraordinary person, with his supportiveness and helpfulness around the house; he and my daughter just took over everything. My business partner was also great about it and didn't object when I bought a couch for my office, so I could lie down sometimes." (Connie and her partner are certified public accountants.)

Eileen, who used to own a small antiques-and-collectibles shop, closed it two and a half years ago, despite her doctor's misgivings: "He warned me, 'Don't live your life around your lupus.' I understand what he meant; he didn't want me thinking like an invalid. Of course he's right, and I don't, really. But I had to be realistic. I knew I just couldn't keep up with running a full-time business and take care of my health at the same time. I'd been having no social life, either."

"This was really the best decision I ever made," she says. "By six months later, I was really feeling much better—I felt I'd gotten control of my life. I decided to use my knowledge and experience to take on a little consulting work—appraisals, that kind of thing; if I worked five hours a week, that was a lot, and I could take naps whenever I wanted. Now, I'm working a bit more, maybe twenty hours a week, and that's just fine. I'm not saving a lot, but my expenses are minimal. My schedule is flexible; sometimes I see three clients in a day, but then I have a day when I can just sleep."

"And," she adds, "I've got time for other things in my life. I've always lived alone, and I've been perfectly happy being single. I never had a burning desire to have children. Well, a few months ago, I was lucky enough to meet a wonderful guy at an art museum I belong to, and we've gotten involved, and that's one of the best things that's happened in my life."

## Get the Endorphins Going

"The biggest change in the way I live since I've known I have lupus," says Nancy, "is that I swim regularly. Before that, I'd been sort of on and off about exercise. I'd be good for a while; then I'd get lazy. But for the past year, I've been swimming as if my life depended on it—and in a way, I feel it does. I hate to say it, but everything they say about exercise is true: I feel more awake; I sleep well; I feel better physically; I'm more alert; I get fewer Raynaud's episodes and fewer flares."

Everything they, and Nancy, say about exercise *is* true, and I would add that for people with lupus who are taking prednisone or another corticosteroid, exercise serves another crucial purpose—promoting muscle strength that can help to counter the skeletal fragility induced by steroid drugs. (See chapter 8 for an in-depth discussion of this subject.)

What kind of exercise is best? It's a highly individual matter, depending on your capabilities and personal preferences, as well as what will fit into your schedule and your life. If you like to exercise in the privacy of your living room, along with one of the popular videotapes, that's fine. Some people find group exercise works best for them, and they attend aerobics classes. If a patient has been very sedentary, I often suggest starting by just walking around the block, once each day; the following week, extend that to twice around the block—or once around *two* blocks. Bicycling is a good, all-around form of exercise. Swimming is excellent, and for those whose joints are often achy, swimming in a heated pool can be a wonderful form of simultaneous exercise and pain relief. If you'd like to begin with a very simple, programmed regimen, see pages 120-131.

Jan has concluded that it's time for her to get some exercise—again: "Three years ago, before the serious joint pains and the fatigue started, I used to go to an aerobics class three times a week. Now, on the Medrol, which gives you a tremendous appetite, I weigh thirty pounds more than I did then. Actually, my weight has gone up and down, and I have a closet full of clothes in I don't know how many different sizes. But I don't have the energy, at this point, to go to an exercise class. My aim, now, is trying to regain some fitness, gradually. I've started with doing some walking each day, and I think there's some improvement; I know I feel a little better."

Elizabeth, too, is a onetime exerciser—in fact, a vigorous one—who's now devised a somewhat less strenuous home program for herself: "I used to take figure-skating classes at a local rink, and after my diagnosis, I kept going, because I could attend an early-morning class. Then the class time changed to mid-afternoon, which would have been impossible, so I gave it up. I also went to a gym, and I did horseback riding, but they got to be too much. But I realized that I wanted and needed some exercise, so I got an exercise bike. I use aerobics tapes, too, and I'm getting a treadmill. My exercise time is when I feel best—the minute I get up in the morning. Then I shower, dress, have breakfast, and I'm all set to get to work."

And Eileen, who's an inveterate biker and hiker, credits a combination of diminished stress, diet-watching, and exercise for the fact that, despite her daily dose of prednisone, not only has she not *gained* weight, she has actually shed some unwanted pounds.

Exercise also increases the release of endorphins. These are substances produced by the brain, and they bind to what we call opiate receptors in other areas of the brain. Those receptors are the same ones that would be targeted if you took an opiate or other powerful pain-killing drug, and the coined name of these substances reflects that; it's short for *endogenous* ("originating within") *morphine*. The endorphins—they're also generated during some other activities, including sex and some forms of meditation—act to diminish physical discomfort by raising the pain threshold, and they also promote a feeling of well-being.

A listing of suggested exercise programs is available from the Arthritis Foundation. Call your local chapter (check the phone directory) or the Foundation's toll-free information line, (800) 283-7800 (Monday through Friday, 9 A.M. to 7 P.M. Eastern time).

## Mind and Body

Rest and exercise can strengthen your body, and better your frame of mind as well. There are also intangible, nonphysical resources to which some have turned with success.

I've mentioned that emotional strains can cause flares. That phenomenon isn't confined to lupus but is characteristic of many chronic conditions. Multiple studies have documented an association between emotionally stressful events and sudden worsening of such disorders as hypertension, heart disease, peptic ulcer, asthma, and diabetes, among others.

The field of psychoimmunology is a young one, and largely unexplored, but we are beginning to understand that the psyche has an impact on the behavior of the immune system (as well as on levels of various hormones), although we have not yet mapped the mechanisms of this influence. Psychosomatic phenomena are very real; the word (which simply means "mind-body") does *not* denote something imaginary or "all in your head," nor does it imply that emotional responses *cause* the disease. Because the term is frequently misunderstood or misused, however, some physicians prefer to talk about "psychological factors affecting physical illness."

Sometimes, the person with lupus makes the connection; that's usually so when the source of the stress is clearly evident—when there has been a major event such as a move to a new home, or a death in the family, for example. But sometimes, she doesn't. Then, professional counseling may be helpful—not to "cope with lupus," which I don't feel generally requires such counseling (although there may be exceptions), but to cope with emotional issues, or reactions to events, that are exacerbating the disease.

I may say to a patient, after we've considered various possibilities that could have triggered a flare—such as other ills (like colds or flu), recent diet departures, major occupational or household changes, physical stresses, and so on—"*Something* is making your lupus worse, and we haven't come up with an explanation. There could be other factors, emotional factors; this can happen in everyone's life. Maybe you would want to explore this." I explain that I'm not suggesting in-depth analysis, or anything long-term, just some help with a temporary problem.

If the patient agrees, I'll recommend someone, a psychiatrist, or, more often, a clinical psychologist. The pairing of personalities is important, since ready communication is crucial, and I ask the patient about any particular preferences—if, for example, the patient might be more comfortable talking with a male therapist or with a female therapist. I also make it clear that the patient should let me know if she decides she doesn't like the person I've recommended. If the referral is going to be helpful, no more than three months of consultation should be needed.

What else can help? As with exercise, whatever works for *you*. Some of my patients swear by transcendental meditation. Some say that spending time in flotation chambers does wonders. Others have ventured into disciplines such as yoga and tai chi and found benefits therein. I can't comment medically on any of these, or advise either for or against them—although any exercise they include, as long as it's not physically stressful, is probably beneficial.

Indeed, according to the Arthritis Foundation, tai chi may be an "ideal" pursuit for those who suffer from arthritis. Developed some 250 years ago as a martial art, tai chi has evolved into a program of slow, gentle movements that only mimic such "fighting" disciplines as kung fu, with priority given to flexibility. The traditional movements may also be altered to accommodate particular physical needs and to avoid stress. Many people, notes the Foundation, find that the discipline offers a form of "moving meditation."

Tai chi is taught in martial-arts schools as well as in many community centers and health clubs.

Jan claims her cats help her cope: "When I'm working, and I start feeling foggy and achy, I get up from the computer and sit down and play with one of the cats for a while. It really helps lift my spirits, and I seem to feel better physically, too."

Maybe it's the break from staring at her computer screen, or just a change of physical position. But maybe not: There has been research demonstrating, among other things, that the presence of pets has helped heart-disease patients live longer, hypertensives lower their blood pressure, and people suffering from depression improve their mood. Some skeptics have suggested that dog-walking and kitten-chasing simply provide healthful exercise—but owners of birds, gerbils, and even iguanas have also been reported to benefit.

Prayer is advocated as a medical modality by some. Mostly, its efficacy has been assessed on a wholly subjective basis; many people employ prayer regarding health, on behalf of themselves or others, and various surveys have found that anywhere from 50 to 70 percent consider it helpful.

One study, however, applied objective standards to the question; the results were reported in the *Southern Medical Journal* in 1988. Over a ten-month period, nearly 400 patients admitted to the coronary-care unit at San Francisco General Hospital, which is affiliated with the University of California, were randomly assigned to an "intercessory prayer" group or a control group, after their permission had been obtained. The study was double-blind, meaning that neither the patients nor their physicians knew to which group each patient was assigned; all the patients in the unit, of course, received the same medical care.

Those in the first group were prayed for every day while they were in the hospital, by a group of born-again Christians outside the hospital who had volunteered to participate in the study. (Some of those in the control group may, of course, have been the subjects of prayer by friends or relatives—but so, probably, were a comparable number of those in the prayer group.) Result: The prayed-for group had a significantly lower "severity score," based on such factors as the development of congestive heart failure or cardiopulmonary arrest, the incidence of pneumonia, and the need for antibiotics.

None of the above, of course, is a substitute for professional medical care—but medicine can't claim to have all the answers, and we shouldn't object to additional therapeutic efforts on the part of patients or others, so long as they cause no harm.

Finally, if you are fortunate enough to have a spouse, "significant other," family member, or friend who has taken the trouble to learn about lupus and offers you informed and concerned support, that can be an extremely important factor for you.

Elizabeth, for one, is convinced it's crucial: "My relationship with my husband has really helped. At one point, I said to him, 'It's hard being sick, but it must be harder living with a sick person.' He said, 'No, I think it must be much harder to be sick.' If it weren't for John, I just couldn't do what I'm doing. Not only does he handle a lot of the cooking. He also does all the errands—food shopping, going to the bank and the post office, whatever needs doing. He's terrific."

Most of those near and dear to you, I hope, will respond that way. Some, unfortunately, don't or, perhaps, can't. There may be others who can provide some of the support you need—and who may benefit from your support as well. See the appendix for a helpful listing.

CHAPTER

# 13

# Lupus in Children and Teens

What I'll be discussing in this chapter is *not* the newborn condition, called "neonatal lupus," which may appear in a small percentage of babies whose mothers have lupus. That condition is strictly transient, and you'll find details in chapter 9 (see page 146).

"Regular" lupus in children and teens, like lupus with onset later in life, is usually a chronic condition. Symptoms, diagnosis, and treatment may differ, although not markedly, from those of the disease when it first appears in the twenties, thirties, and forties. There may also be significant emotional impact, not only upon the growing child but upon other family members, siblings in particular. I hope this chapter will help parents (and some siblings) of youngsters with lupus understand and cope with this condition and its attendant concerns.

## The Statistical Picture

Although not unheard of, lupus appearing before the age of five is extremely rare. After that age, the incidence gradually increases year by year through adolescence.

As in adults, more young females than males are afflicted by lupus, although the differences are far less dramatic. The ratio of girls to boys up to age ten is about three to one, according to most studies (some have estimated a lower ratio); that rises to six to one among adolescents.

There appears to be an even stronger familial association in child-onset lupus than with onset in adulthood. An estimated 27 percent of the children—more than a quarter—have an affected first- or second-degree relative. Among children with lupus, a third of their parents and 39 percent of their sisters have tested positive for antinuclear antibodies (ANA).

The concordance rate among identical twins—the occurrence of lupus in both twins—among children has been reported, in various studies, to range from 57 to 69 percent, a substantially higher proportion than that seen in adults. As I noted in chapter 3, some studies in adults have put the figure as low as 20 percent.

The higher concordance is not unexpected, and it tends to support prevailing theory as to a genetic factor in lupus. Childhood twins—living in the same household, often sleeping in the same room, eating the same food, attending school together, and sharing other activities—are far more likely to be mutually exposed to the same viruses, the same air pollutants, and so on than adult twins. If lupus is triggered by a combination of genetic and environmental factors, that combination is much more likely to occur in childhood than later.

When both of a set of identical twins have lupus, though, it doesn't necessarily appear at the same time. In most cases, the second twin to develop the disease will do so within about three and a half years, but reported intervals have ranged up to fourteen years.

## Signs and Symptoms

Arthritis and rashes are among the most common first signals of lupus in adults, and that's true in children as well. Most have a rash of some sort. Many complain of joint discomfort, and the joints may also be stiff and swollen.

About 50 percent of children—a somewhat higher proportion than among adults—have the classic butterfly rash across the nose and cheeks; some studies have reported a proportion as high as 75 percent. Other skin symptoms may include lesions of the discoid type (uncommon in children), crusty or scaly lesions (often mainly on the upper part of the body), and simple redness.

In youngsters, though, fever is also a major symptom—in fact, the most common. Overall, about 75 percent have an elevated temperature at the time of diagnosis; in some studies, the figures have been 90 to 100 percent.

Among other frequent symptoms are muscle aches, thinning hair or change in hair texture (it may become brittle), and enlarged lymph nodes ("swollen glands") in the neck, armpits, and/or groin. Still other symptoms may include poor appetite with consequent weight loss, headache, fatigue, Raynaud's phenomenon, and gastrointestinal problems. Children appear to be at greater risk than adults for kidney complications, and there is a higher incidence, among children with lupus, of blood abnormalities such as thrombocytopenia and hemolytic anemia.

Children are subject to a host of infections and other disorders, and there is great potential for misdiagnosis. In one series of forty-some children with lupus described in the medical literature in the late 1960s, fully half had first been thought to have some other disease, often acute rheumatic fever (the diagnosis given for one in four) or rheumatoid arthritis. Other initial diagnoses that have been mistakenly applied to youngsters later diagnosed with lupus include kidney infection, leukemia, epilepsy, mononucleosis, rubella, and infectious arthritis.

## Diagnostic Determinants

Lupus in children is now much less likely to be confused with infections, cancers, and other conditions. Early and accurate diagnosis is now the norm, due to a number of factors, including the decreasing frequency of rheumatic fever,[*] vastly improved laboratory testing and, not least, the heightened realization among pediatricians and family physicians that lupus can and does occur in children.

No special tests or other standards are employed in diagnosing youngsters. The American College of Rheumatology (ACR) diagnostic criteria—which I enumerated in chapter 2—are applied to children as well. In children as in adults, there are many cases of lupus that do not technically meet the official criteria, and other observations will also be taken into account. Reported results on key laboratory tests show no significant differences between children and adults.

---

[*] Rheumatic fever may occur as a sequel to a number of infections caused by streptococcal bacteria ("strep"), including pneumonia, strep sore throat, scarlet fever, tonsillitis, and some ear infections—*if* the infection has been untreated or improperly treated. Since successful treatment with effective antibiotics is now the norm, rheumatic fever has become uncommon.

# Lupus Treatment in Children

It is best for a child with lupus to be treated by a pediatric rheumatologist, a subspecialist who is familiar not only with the disease but with children—and the ramifications of the disease in someone who is at the same time growing, developing, and changing both physiologically and psychologically.

Most of the same modalities used to treat lupus in adults are also used in therapy for youngsters—and, as with adults, the disease is unpredictable and treatment must be highly individualized to fit each young patient's situation.

Mild disease, manifested mostly by fever and minor aches and pains, can often be managed with a regular regimen of nonsteroidal anti-inflammatory drugs (NSAIDs), whether salicylates (aspirin and related drugs) or one of the many prescription medications. Hydroxychloroquine may be given for rashes and other symptoms. More serious or persistent symptoms may call for one of the corticosteroids, or even an immunosuppressant. All of these standard lupus drugs are discussed in detail in chapters 5 and 6.

Most of the complications I discussed in chapter 7, ranging from anemia to kidney dysfunction, may occur in children—indeed, aseptic necrosis of bone has been reported to occur more often among youngsters taking corticosteroids than among adults—and the same recourses apply.

Many children with lupus are sun-sensitive—the rate may be twice as high among children as among adults—and this becomes a special concern for parents, since children spend so much more time out of doors than adults. In individuals who are photosensitive, light can set off not only skin reactions but systemic flares as well, so that—difficult as it may be—restrictions need to be imposed on amount of time spent outside and preventive measures taken, like using sunscreen. See the guidelines on this subject in chapter 11, as well as the advice there on dental care and heart lesions, and on Sjögren's syndrome, if they apply to your child.

Parents should be aware that, as with adults, the prognosis for children with lupus has vastly improved over the past two to three decades. The survival figures are similar to those of adults, and some leading medical centers now report ten-year survival rates that approach 100 percent.

## Standard Preventives

The major threat is often not lupus itself but infection, which is the most common cause of death in children with lupus. Children who have lupus are especially susceptible to infections if they are taking high doses of certain drugs. A sudden fever should alert a parent to a problem—which may be an infection, a flare of lupus, or something else; the bottom line is that the doctor should be called without delay.

It's important to realize that steroids, and immunosuppressants such as cyclophosphamide, lower the body's ability to resist infection. This means, for one thing, that it's vital for your child to receive all recommended childhood immunizations. Recommendations are established by the Immunization Practices Advisory Committee of the Centers for Disease Control and Prevention (CDC) and the American Academy of Pediatrics Committee on Infectious Diseases.

The present guidelines for routine childhood immunization include the following:

- Hepatitis B vaccine—the first shot is given before the newborn goes home from the hospital, the second at two months, and a third some time between six and eighteen months.

- The DTP (sometimes DPT) shot, an injection that protects against diphtheria, tetanus, and pertussis (whooping cough). It's given at the ages of two, four, and six months, at about a year and a half, and again at four to six years. After that, there should be a Td shot (the designation for the adult formulation, which drops the pertussis component) every ten years—at age fifteen, at twenty-five, and so on.

- OPV, oral polio vaccine, given at two and four months and again at about fifteen to eighteen months.

- *Haemophilus influenzae* type b conjugate vaccine (HbCV), sometimes called "the Hib shot." This vaccine—actually three slightly different vaccines have been licensed—protects against infection with a bacterium (it has no connection with flu, which is caused by a virus) that can cause a number of critical illnesses; it is the most common cause of bacterial meningitis in this country. The schedule of injections starts at two months and may vary thereafter depending upon the brand of vaccine used; there will be a total of either three or four shots, with the last one given at either twelve or fifteen months.

- MMR, the measles-mumps-rubella shot—the first one at fifteen months, the second at either four or five years or later at eleven or twelve. The variation in the second shot is dictated by local regulations and / or disease patterns where you live. In high-risk areas, the vaccine may be given at one year; or a measles shot alone may be given even earlier (the MMR is still given at fifteen months).

Your physician may suggest departures from this schedule; the reasons may include lupus complications, other illness, or a regimen of high-dosage steroids. Of course, his or her advice should be followed. More important than the specific times mentioned (which are geared to the usual standard checkup visits during the first year) are the total number of doses and the intervals between them—so that if one shot in a series is postponed, the next one may also be postponed if there would otherwise be an unacceptably short time between shots.

If you've realized, after reading the above rundown, that your child has missed any required immunizations, talk to your doctor about setting up a catch-up schedule.

## Special Precautions

Your youngster's medications may mean that two other particular infections pose special risks: influenza (flu) and chickenpox. There are hazards involving two kinds of medications.

Corticosteroids and other immunosuppressants create the same problem as they do with the other infections I've mentioned: The immune system cannot mount an adequate defense against the infection. Critical complications could ensue from these usually relatively mild illnesses. Chickenpox could result in such life-threatening conditions as pneumonia, pancreatitis, hepatitis, or encephalitis.

The second peril is posed by aspirin. A rare but potentially lethal condition, called Reye's (pronounced "ryes") syndrome, affects children and teens and has been found to occur disproportionately often following a bout of flu or chickenpox during which the child took aspirin. Since the mid-1980s, the U.S. Food and Drug Administration (FDA) has required that aspirin and products containing it bear labels warning that they should not be given to children and teenagers with those ills, and since then the incidence of Reye's syndrome has dropped markedly.

If your child is already taking aspirin, this dangerous combination must be avoided by making an effort to avoid flu and chickenpox.

So far as flu is concerned, that means the youngster should receive vaccine. The shots are needed annually and, since the several flu viruses mutate frequently, the vaccine is reformulated each year to incorporate all the currently circulating strains. The flu season generally runs from December through March, and November is the ideal time for shots, since the protection lasts only a few months. It's probably a good idea for the entire family to have them.

At this writing, a chickenpox vaccine is under consideration for approval by the FDA, and such a vaccine may have become available by the time you read this. (It will probably become part of the routine childhood vaccination schedule.) If so, your child or teenager who has not had chickenpox, and who takes aspirin, or steroids or other immunosuppressant drugs, should be vaccinated. If no vaccine is yet available, three other precautions can be taken:

1. Try to see that the child is not exposed to anyone with the virus. If chickenpox is running rampant at your child's school, it's wise for the child to stay home for a while.

2. If your child is exposed to chickenpox—*or* to an adult with shingles—contact your doctor immediately. The FDA advises that the child should receive VZIG ("vee-zig"), varicella-zoster immune globulin. The varicella-zoster virus causes chickenpox, medically termed varicella. It also causes shingles (medically termed herpes zoster), which is caused by a reactivation of the virus in someone who has had chickenpox.

VZIG was developed in the 1970s by the CDC. It is one of a number of specific immune globulins that confer "passive immunization." Vaccines—"active immunization"—work by introducing bacteria or a virus, thereby stimulating the body to produce antibodies against the particular infectious agent. Immune globulins, derived from immune plasma, already contain such antibodies, produced by other people in response to viral challenge. VZIG, like most immune globulins, is given by intramuscular injection.

In case you wonder why all children shouldn't receive VZIG to fight off chickenpox: Its impact is limited. Vaccines confer duration of immunity equal to having the disease itself, which varies from one disease to another. VZIG provides protection that lasts only about three months.

3. If your child who is taking any of these drugs actually comes down with chickenpox—again, contact your doctor immediately. The recourse is a drug, acyclovir (Zovirax), which was approved by the FDA in early 1992 for the treatment of chickenpox. (It had previously received approval for the treatment of some other viral infections.)

The drug is available in both oral and injectable forms. If a child is immunocompromised—is taking steroids or other immunosuppressant drugs—and comes down with chickenpox, FDA experts say that the drug should be administered by intravenous injection, since pneumonia could develop rapidly. They also point out that the bioavailability of the oral form—the degree to which it is actually usable by the body—is lower.[*]

---

[*]Oral acyclovir, while not appropriate to counter the threat posed by immunosuppression, shortens the course of chickenpox a little and diminishes the number of skin lesions. It may be used for teenagers who come down with the disease, since they seem to get a lot sicker than younger children. It may also be prescribed for the second child in a household who gets chickenpox; that child, for unknown reasons, is frequently sicker (not in a life-threatening sense, but in terms of discomfort).

I want to emphasize the word *immediately*, which I've used in talking about calling your doctor. Time is truly of the essence. If your child has been exposed to, or comes down with, chickenpox, the appropriate measures must be taken *very quickly* to prevent complications.

## Psychological and Emotional Concerns

The following is from a letter I received from a woman who had read my earlier book on lupus:

> My daughter, age 15, was just recently diag-
> nosed with lupus. She is now taking
> prednisone tablets. Her joints are hurting, she
> has anemia, and our doctor has warned us
> that her spleen will have to be removed. But
> our main problem is that my daughter's
> emotions and temperament have changed,
> and we are having a very difficult time
> handling this. Can you suggest anything that
> will help us?

Adolescents go through some very complicated experiences in many areas, including psychological and sexual maturation, social adaptation, and physical growth and development. It doesn't help to have a chronic illness, one that causes physical discomfort and is often unpredictable—and, in this case, includes the prospect of major surgery—superimposed on all that. And this understandably upset young girl had not yet encountered prednisone's adverse effects; in adolescence, in addition to those I detailed in chapter 6, they can include severe acne and obesity, as well as (temporarily) delayed growth and slowed sexual maturation.

What I suggested to the mother who wrote me is that she seek emotional support for both herself and her daughter. I suggested that she contact her local chapter of the Lupus Foundation (see the appendix). I urged her to talk to her daughter's rheumatologist about her concerns as well, knowing that this might result in a referral for counseling.

With younger children, the problem is usually a little different. While teens may take on a new psychic burden, the main problem with younger children is often that they have no realization of the nature and seriousness of their illness. Especially when it is under control and they have no discomfort, they are heedless of the need for basic health-maintenance measures (eating properly to prevent nutritional deficiencies, dental hygiene, and so on), as well as special precautions such as avoidance of overexposure to the sun—not to mention following a necessary medication regimen. That heedlessness is normal for kids, of course. Parents need to take extra care, when a child has lupus, to be sure the health rules are followed.

And do be prepared for personality changes. A young child who has a chronic illness may become difficult and demanding. A young child *or* teen may also react with rage, resentment, and rebellion—which may result, depending on the child's age and capacities, in behavior ranging from minor naughtiness to sexual promiscuity, habitual illicit drug use, and other antisocial acting-out.

It might be wise to anticipate such reactions by seeking "prophylactic" psychological or psychiatric counseling, with a view to heading off incipient problems. If this is done before any problems arise, it need not appear to the child that such counseling is in any way a "punishment," or that the youngster has done anything "wrong." A visit or visits to a counselor can be presented simply as consultation with another doctor, who will bring another point of view to dealing with the illness of which the child is already aware; your pediatrician or family physician may be able to offer the best advice about such consultation. If a youngster can share his or her feelings about having this complex and confusing disease, perhaps those feelings can be steered into constructive channels before they explode.

Regardless of the ages of your children, if you have more than one, you need to think, too, about the impact of the illness on the lupus patient's sibling(s) and on the relationship between them—as well as your relationship with your well child(ren).

Remember, worried as you are about the child with lupus, and anxious as you are to take the necessary time to care for that child's special needs, the healthy child has needs as well. That child needs to know that your love and concern have not lessened because a sibling is ill. And remember that lupus is a chronic condition; this is usually not a temporary situation. Your child who has lupus needs to know that the illness does not and will not mean that the child deserves, or will receive, your exclusive attention.

Within the limits dictated by age, siblings should be given information about the disease, and its symptoms—which may be frightening or simply bewildering—should be explained. Young children sometimes view illness as a sort of stigma; they need to be assured that the sick child is not bad, is not being punished, and is not "abnormal." Do all you can to encourage them to continue to play and spend time together. Unless your doctor has advised you otherwise, there is no reason a child with lupus cannot (with sensible precautions such as sun protection) participate in sports and other normal childhood activities.

If you believe you see problems developing, you might want to ask your physician for referral to a child psychiatrist or psychologist, or to a family therapist, for counseling.

# 14

# New Directions, Future Therapies

A number of potential therapies for severe lupus have been under study and have stimulated interest among rheumatologists. Whether or not they will prove beneficial remains to be seen.

## Plasmapheresis

One such therapy is a technique called plasmapheresis. First proposed in the mid-1970s as a possible treatment for lupus, it's based on a principle similar to that of dialysis, in which blood is circulated outside the body and potentially toxic waste materials are filtered out, a process that is normally handled by the kidneys.

Plasma, which constitutes about 50 percent of the blood, is the fluid in which the blood cells—red cells, white cells, and thrombocytes (platelets)—are suspended. *Pheresis* is the medical term (from the Greek *aphairesis*, "removal") for any procedure in which blood is withdrawn, a specific part of its content removed, and the remainder returned to the body. In plasmapheresis, a quantity of plasma is removed and replaced by an inert colloid solution.

This procedure temporarily reduces the amount of antibodies, antigen-antibody complexes, and other troublemakers circulating through the bloodstream. In clinical trials, it has been performed several times a week over a period of weeks, accompanied or followed by administration of the immunosuppressant agent cyclophosphamide or that drug in combination with prednisone.

The technique has also been tried in rheumatoid arthritis and has been found to afford some relief from pain and disability in that disease, although the effect has been short-lived.

As for lupus: While some physicians believe that plasmapheresis holds promise for the treatment of severe glomerulonephritis and other acute complications of lupus, many find the evidence thus far unconvincing.

Results of the largest recent study, reported in the spring of 1992—a broad, controlled trial undertaken by researchers at fourteen medical centers—were disappointing. Comparison of patients receiving prednisone plus short-term administration of cyclophosphamide with a group receiving the same regimen plus plasmapheresis showed that improvement of renal disease occurred at about the same rate in both groups. There were, in fact, slightly more deaths and cases of renal failure in the plasmapheresis group, although the differences weren't statistically significant. The investigators concluded that the technique effected no improvement in clinical outcome and that they could not recommend the treatment.

It must be noted, however, that the trial was a lengthy one and had begun in the early 1980s. At that time, precise protocols were established as to therapy regimens—dosages of drugs, schedules, and so on. Some rheumatologists have suggested that concepts of the workings of the immune system have changed radically over the intervening decade, and have argued that present knowledge might dictate different—and possibly more effective—use of plasmapheresis.

A group of German researchers reported in late 1992 on a small pilot study of plasmapheresis followed by high-dose cyclophosphamide, followed in turn by oral cyclophosphamide and prednisone. Eight of fourteen patients had gone into treatment-free remission. (The patients had been followed for an average of two and one half years at the time of the report.) The method used by these investigators is now under study at a number of medical centers in several countries.

## Total Lymphoid Irradiation

In another experimental technique, known as total lymphoid irradiation (TLI), radiation is carefully beamed to lymph nodes and other tissues where lymphocytes—the white blood cells that generate antibodies—congregate. TLI has been used for many years in treating Hodgkin's disease and other forms of lymphoma (malignancies involving the lymph system), and it has been found both safe and effective in those conditions.

Clinical studies in lupus patients have been limited, but thus far it appears that TLI suppresses antibody production that relies on helper T-cells, resulting in diminished levels of ANA and anti-DNA antibodies. One drawback appears to be the possibility of increased susceptibility to minor bacterial infections.

There is an advantage, however, in TLI over taking a drug such as cyclophosphamide, which can induce sterility. This advantage was cited by Stanford University researchers who compared the two treatments and reported their results at the 1992 American College of Rheumatology meeting. In their patients, the therapies proved equally effective for nephritis, and two of twenty-two women who received TLI subsequently became pregnant; both pregnancies resulted in normal, healthy babies.

## Monoclonal Antibodies

There is a new therapy that has been studied for a number of years in the mice that have served as laboratory "models" of human lupus, but has only recently begun to be examined in humans.

The administration to these mice of antibodies to gene products of the mouse major histocompatibility complex, the mouse counterpart of the HLA locus in humans (see page 40), has been shown to suppress several forms of autoimmune disease, including the mouse equivalent of lupus. These antibodies are known as *monoclonal* antibodies, because each is derived—cloned—from a single antibody-producing cell. A significant obstacle has been potential adverse effects on protective immunity, that is, defense against disease.

Alternative strategies being pursued in the mouse studies include devising antibodies targeted only to specific, active "helper" T-cells, or to the busiest B-cells, with the aim of putting autoimmune mechanisms out of commission while sparing the normal, protective capability of the immune system.

There have also been some very small studies, using the approach of directing antibodies against specific immune-system cells, in human lupus patients, but administration of antibody to a particular class of "helper" T-cells (CD4+ cells) does not appear to depress the population of those cells for very long at all. Some researchers have suggested that the approach might be combined with corticosteroid therapy for enhanced effectiveness.

## Hormones and Anti-Hormones

With the prominence of lupus in women and major incidence during the childbearing years, there has, of course, been sustained interest in the role played by hormones in general, and estrogens and other reproductive hormones in particular.

If estrogens encourage lupus, might androgens discourage the disease?

In one of the experimental lupus "models"—the NZW / NZB mice (New Zealand white and black strains)—it's been demonstrated that proteinuria and the incidence of nephritis can be decreased in mice treated with androgens. This concept has led to some very small trials in human lupus patients, but the effects of administering androgens to women, to date, have been inconclusive.

A drug called danazol (Danocrine, Cyclomen), a synthetic androgen derivative, has also been considered. It is an inhibitor of certain pituitary hormones and is believed to suppress the production of some ovarian hormones; it has been used in the treatment of endometriosis, a proliferation of endometrial (uterine lining) tissue outside the uterus.

In a study reported in 1992, the drug did not seem to be ideal. Among a group of two dozen patients, in terms of the prevalence of arthritis and rashes, as well as hemolytic anemia and some blood tests, the drug did appear promising. But in more serious considerations, such as kidney complications, there was no benefit. And the researchers commented that the condition of all the male patients in the clinical trial (four of the twenty-four) worsened.

I mentioned at the end of chapter 11 that tamoxifen, an "anti-estrogen" drug usually used to treat breast cancer, appears paradoxically to maintain bone density; hence it has been viewed as an alternative to estrogen replacement. Because it *does* oppose estrogen, it has also been automatically placed on the list of potential anti-lupus agents. Thus far, the concept has been applied only to the lupus-afflicted experimental mice. In the latest study, reported at the American College of Rheumatology meeting in 1992, effects in the mice were described as "remarkable." Side effects were not detailed.

Observations in one of the experimental mouse strains have suggested that prolactin may be associated with increased severity of lupus. Prolactin is a hormone, secreted by the pituitary gland at the base of the brain. It is produced in particularly high quantities during pregnancy and following childbirth, when it stimulates breast enlargement and milk production (lactation); it is also known as lactogenic hormone. (The hormone is produced by both sexes but appears to have no significant role in males.)

When extra pituitary glands were implanted in female mice with lupus, raising their blood levels of prolactin, they became much sicker. Conversely, when they were given a drug, bromocriptine, which acts to inhibit release of prolactin by the pituitary, the result was better health and increased longevity.[*]

---

[*] Bromocriptine (Parlodel) was introduced in the late 1970s for the treatment of certain cases of infertility in which absence of menstruation and ovulation is associated with high blood prolactin levels not due to pituitary microadenomas (tiny, benign tumors which can cause overproduction of the hormone).

# A Traditional Chinese Remedy

We have in recent years come to realize that modern science does not have a monopoly on healing—that folk remedies handed down from ages past, often based on particular plants associated with curative powers, may have something to offer as well. Indeed, some of our best-known medications are derived from plants, including the heart drug digitalis, from the leaves of *Digitalis purpurea*, the purple foxglove; the gout medicine colchicine, from the seeds of *Colchicum*, the meadow saffron; and the anticancer agent vincristine, from *Vinca rosea*, the Madagascar periwinkle.

There was notable interest at the 1992 international lupus conference in London in research being carried out on the Asian shrub *Tripterygium wilfordii* (various plants of this genus are native to Japan, Korea, and parts of China), which furnishes a traditional Chinese remedy. The medication is in current use there for the treatment of lupus, rheumatoid arthritis, and other autoimmune disorders.

An extract from the plant appears to be highly beneficial in mice with lupus, and one Shanghai Medical University researcher reported that, in a group of 200-plus human lupus patients, the extract performed on a par with corticosteroids, and a combination of the extract with corticosteroids seemed a little more effective than either used alone. The extract appears, according to the researcher, to have an anti-inflammatory effect similar to that of the corticosteroids.

A Canadian research team has also worked with the Tripterygium extract in the model mice. Investigators from McGill University in Montreal said at a 1992 American College of Rheumatology meeting that treated mice had less severe arthritis and glomerulonephritis, a decrease in proteinuria, and a significantly longer life span, despite the fact that levels of autoantibodies didn't change.

University of California scientists who have analyzed the medication and confirmed its immunosuppressant effects in the laboratory also described their work at the ACR meeting.

## Cyclosporin

Immunosuppressants—notably, cyclophosphamide and the large family of corticosteroids—have been broadly employed in the treatment of lupus. Another drug that falls into that category, but hasn't been widely considered until recently, is one called cyclosporin. Its main use has been in staving off the ravages of rejection of transplanted organs. It would seem logical, therefore, that it might be deemed a possibility for treatment of overenthusiastic immune reactions such as occur in lupus.

Tentative clinical trials in lupus, in the early 1980s, were not promising. While the drug proved effective in joint-pain relief, there was a high incidence of unacceptable side effects, including nausea, vomiting, hair loss and, most disturbing, kidney problems. More recently, other research groups have reported results of clinical investigations with the drug. Again, kidney insufficiency has been a continuing concern, along with liver and other problems, and some of the studies revealed a higher incidence of side effects than others.

The consensus appears to be a qualified "not yet."

# Appendix:
# Good Connections (You're Not Alone)

We don't know exactly how many people with lupus there are, either in this country or worldwide, but in the United States alone there may be a million—or *more*. You can be sure, wherever you live, that there are other lupus patients not too far away. Many find it helpful to touch base with others, to exchange information and to share problems and solutions.

Sometimes small groups of patients get together under the leadership or guidance of a physician, social worker, psychologist, or other experienced counselor. Informal groups like this often spring from a single group of patients, such as those attending a particular clinic.

## One to One

In New York City, there is a program that's been in operation for several years; it may soon be available elsewhere in the country as well.

In 1988, the social-work department at The Hospital for Special Surgery in New York City, which houses the orthopedics and rheumatology divisions of the New York Hospital-Cornell Medical Center, in collaboration with New York's S.L.E. Foundation, opened the LupusLine. It's not a "hot line" or an emergency number, and it doesn't dispense medical advice. Rather, the callers—often, patients who have recently been diagnosed, or who have encountered a problem—are seeking practical answers.

"Newly diagnosed patients," explains Roberta Horton, the program's director, "are often uncertain and anxious about the impact of their disease on their lives—on their marriage, their kids, their jobs. New mothers are worried about infant care. Patients are concerned about how to explain symptoms like the terrible fatigue to others."

Obviously, the people who can best answer these questions are those who have successfully coped with the very same questions themselves, and have done so successfully, and that is indeed the principle of the LupusLine. Callers are put in touch with such individuals, called peer counselors, on a one-to-one basis, in a sort of "buddy system" that operates via telephone, home to home. This quick connection is a distinct advantage, Horton points out, for busy people (both counselors and counseled) who haven't time to attend meetings of support groups—or who simply dislike groups, for one reason or another.

The peer counselors are all volunteers; often, they are recommended by their own physicians, who feel that they're the kind of people whose knowledge, empathy, communications skills, and sense of responsibility suggest that they could help others.

They attend several weeks of training before they join the program, as well as monthly update seminars at which new information about lupus is presented and counselors exchange (anonymous) case information from the logs they're required to keep.

"The counselors often benefit from the program themselves," says Horton. "There's a great sense of accomplishment in being able to help others by sharing what they've learned."

At this writing, groups in other communities around the country have expressed interest in setting up their own LupusLines, and Horton and her staff have developed a comprehensive training manual based on the New York LupusLine experience. The Lupus Foundation of America (see below) has also provided research funding for the program.

The New York LupusLine's number is (212) 606-1952.

## A Helpful Network

Jan went to a meeting sponsored by the group in her area and experienced a revelation: "You read about rashes and lupus and all you see mentioned is either that famous butterfly rash or the discoid kind. I walked into this room and saw fifty women with my complexion. I now realize that a lupus 'rash' can just be like a sort of blush with dryness, not necessarily a full-blown rash at all."

Lisa connected with the group in her area not long after she found out she had lupus and, as a result, "Every once in a while, if they think I can help, they ask me to talk with newly diagnosed patients."

There are two national voluntary health organizations that concern themselves with lupus. One is the Arthritis Foundation (1314 Spring Street NW, Atlanta GA 30309), which addresses not only arthritis per se but the entire spectrum of rheumatic diseases. It supports research and publishes informative advisories for both physicians and the public on all of these disorders, which include not only lupus and related conditions but a host of others ranging from rheumatoid arthritis to infectious arthritis, osteoarthritis, Lyme disease, and gout.

The other organization, with which readers of this book are likely to identify more closely, is the Lupus Foundation of America (LFA), which focuses solely on lupus. The groups mentioned by Jan and Lisa are local chapters of the Foundation.

The national organization funds research and seeks generally to educate professionals, patients, and the public. It publishes excellent brochures on the various aspects of lupus, as well as a three-times-a-year newsletter, *Lupus News*, which offers both scientific and practical, patient-oriented information. LFA is at 4 Research Place, Suite 180, Rockville MD 20850 and may be reached at either (301) 670-9292 or (800) 558-0121.

Lisa and Jan are members of LFA local chapters (all individual memberships are through the chapters rather than directly with the national group). The chapters make LFA literature available to both members and nonmembers, hold seminars and other meetings, and fund local projects (as noted, the LupusLine in New York has received funding from the S.L.E. Foundation, the Manhattan LFA chapter). Many also publish their own newsletters and sponsor support groups, as well as subchapters and branches.

LFA chapters are currently active in all but five states; there are, as yet, no chapters in Oregon, Washington State, Wyoming, or either of the Dakotas. Here, for your reference, is a state-by-state rundown. Readers in the Dakotas, see the Minnesota listing; readers in Oregon and Washington should call California, and those in Wyoming should call Colorado.

# Alabama

LFA, Birmingham Chapter
4 Office Park Circle, Suite 302
Birmingham AL 35223
(205) 870-0504

LFA, Montgomery Chapter
P.O. Box 11507
Montgomery AL 36111
(205) 288-3032

# Alaska

LFA, Alaska Chapter
P.O. Box 211336
Anchorage AK 99521
(907) 338-6332

# Arizona

LFA, Greater Arizona Chapter
2149 West Indian School Road
Phoenix AZ 85015
(602) 266-7970

LFA, Southern Arizona Chapter
3113 East First Street, Suite C
Tucson AZ 85716
(602) 327-9922

# Arkansas

LFA, Fort Smith Chapter
P.O. Box 6340
Fort Smith AR 72906
(918) 427-6302

# California

Bay Area L.E. Foundation
2635 North First Street, Suite 206
San Jose CA 95134
(408) 954-8600 or
(800) 523-3363 (CA only)

LFA, Southern California Chapter
14600 Goldenwest Street, #104
Westminster CA 92683
(714) 891-6400 or
(800) 426-6026 (CA only)

# Colorado

Lupus Foundation of Colorado
Villa Italia Offices
7200 West Alameda
Lakewood CO 80226
(303) 922-5123 (hotline) or -5259 or
(800) 858-1292 (CO only)

# Connecticut

LFA, Connecticut Chapter
45 South Main Street, Room 208
West Hartford CT 06107
(203) 521-9151

# Delaware

LFA, Delaware Chapter
P.O. Box 6391
Wilmington DE 19804
(302) 999-8686

# District of Columbia area

Lupus Foundation of Greater
   Washington
515-A Braddock Road, 2C
Alexandria VA 22314
(703) 684-2925

# Florida

LFA, Southeast Florida Chapter
   Southern Unit
2845 Aventura Boulevard
North Miami Beach FL 33180
(305) 931-1407 or
(800) 339-0586

LFA, Southeast Florida Chapter
Northern Unit
P.O. Box 18645
24005 Mercer Avenue, Suite 6
West Palm Beach FL 33401
(407) 655-1252

LFA, Brevard County Chapter
P.O. Box 372909
Satellite Beach FL 32937
(407) 768-9401

LFA, Northwest Florida Chapter
P.O. Box 17841
Pensacola FL 32522
(904) 444-7070

LFA, Tampa Area Chapter
4579 Gunn Highway
Tampa FL 33624
(813) 960-3992 or
(800) 330-3992 (FL only)

Lupus Foundation of Florida
4406 Urban Court
Orlando FL 32810
(407) 295-8500

LFA, North Florida Chapter
P.O. Box 10486
Jacksonville FL 32247
(904) 387-4470

LFA, Suncoast Chapter
P.O. Box 23244
St. Petersburg FL 33742
(813) 522-4892

## Georgia

LFA, Columbus Chapter
233 Twelfth Street, Suite 819
Columbus GA 31901
(706) 571-8950

LFA, Greater Atlanta Chapter
340 Interstate North Parkway NW,
Suite 455
Atlanta GA 30339
(404) 952-3891 or
(800) 800-4532 (GA only)

LFA, Savannah Chapter
P.O. Box 2532
Savannah GA 31402
(912) 354-5106

## Hawaii

Hawaii Lupus Foundation
1200 College Walk Street, Suite 114
Honolulu HI 96817
(808) 538-1522

## Idaho

Idaho Lupus Support Group
4696 Overland Road, Suite 512
Boise ID 83705
(208) 343-4907

## Illinois

LFA, Illinois Chapter
P.O. Box 42812
Chicago IL 60642
(312) 779-3181 or
(800) 258-7872 (IL only)

LFA, Danville Chapter
322 East 13 Street
Danville IL 61832
(217) 446-7672

## Indiana

Indiana Lupus Foundation
2701 East Southport Road
Indianapolis IN 46227
(317) 783-6033

LFA, Northeast Indiana Chapter
5401 Keystone Drive, Suite 202
Fort Wayne IN 46825
(219) 482-8205

LFA, Northwest Indiana Chapter
3819 West 40 Avenue
Gary IN 46408
(219) 980-4826

## Iowa

LFA, Iowa Chapter
P.O. Box 36034
Des Moines IA 50312
(515) 285-8413

## Kansas

LFA, Wichita Chapter
P.O. Box 16094
Wichita KS 67216
(316) 262-6180

## Kentucky

Lupus Foundation of Kentuckiana
1850 Bluegrass Avenue
Louisville KY 40215
(502) 366-9681

## Louisiana

Louisiana Lupus Foundation
7732 Goodwood Boulevard, #B
Baton Rouge LA 70806
(504) 927-8052

LFA, Centa Chapter
P.O. Box 12565
Alexandria LA 71315
(318) 473-0125

LFA, Northeast Louisiana Chapter
102 Susan Drive
West Monroe LA 71291
(318) 396-1333

LFA, Shreveport Chapter
1961 Bayou Drive
Shreveport LA 71105
(318) 861-4862

## Maine

LFA, Maine Chapter
P.O. Box 8168
Portland ME 04104
(207) 878-8104

## Maryland

Maryland Lupus Foundation
7400 York Road, Third Floor
Baltimore MD 21204
(410) 337-9000 or
(800) 777-0934 (MD only)

## Massachusetts

LFA, Massachusetts Chapter
425 Watertown Street
Newton MA 02158
(617) 332-9014

## Michigan

Michigan Lupus Foundation
26202 Harper Avenue
St. Clair Shores MI 48081
(313) 775-8310

## Minnesota

LFA, Minnesota Chapter
International Market Square
275 Market Street, C-17
Minneapolis MN 55405
(612) 375-1131 or
(800) 645-1131 (MN, ND, SD only)

## Mississippi

LFA, Mississippi Chapter
P.O. Box 24292
Jackson MS 39225
(601) 366-5655

## Missouri

LFA, Kansas City Chapter
10804 Fremont Avenue
Kansas City MO 64134
(816) 765-3887

LFA, Ozarks Chapter
3150 West Marty Street
Springfield MO 65807
(417) 887-1560

LFA, Missouri Chapter
8420 Delmar Boulevard, #LL1
St. Louis MO 63124
(314) 432-0008

## Montana

LFA, Montana Chapter
1517 14th Street West, Suite 213
Billings MT 59102
(406) 256-5262

## Nebraska

LFA, Omaha Chapter
Community Healthy Plaza
7101 Newport Avenue, #310
Omaha NE 68152
(402) 572-3150

LFA, Western Nebraska Chapter
HCR 72, Box 58
Sutherland NE 69165
(308) 764-2474

## Nevada

LFA, Las Vegas Chapter
1555 East Flamingo, Suite 439
Las Vegas NV 89119
(702) 369-0474

LFA, Northern Nevada Chapter
1755 Vassar Street
Reno NV 89502
(702) 323-2444

## New Hampshire

LFA, New Hampshire Chapter
P.O. Box 444
Nashua NH 03061
(603) 424-5668

## New Jersey

LFA, South Jersey Chapter
Starrett Building
6 White Horse Pike, #1-C
Haddon Heights NJ 08035
(609) 546-8555

Lupus Foundation of New Jersey
287 Market Street, P.O. Box 320
Elmwood Park NJ 07407
(201) 791-7868

## New Mexico

LFA, New Mexico Chapter
P.O. Box 35891
Albuquerque NM 87176
(505) 881-9081

## New York

LFA, Bronx Chapter
P.O. Box 1117
Bronx NY 10462
(718) 822-6542

LFA, Central New York Chapter
Maria Regina Center,
    Building B
1118 Court Street
Syracuse NY 13208
(315) 472-6011

LFA, Genesee Valley Chapter
P.O. Box 14068
Rochester NY 14614
(716) 381-2790

LFA, Long Island/Queens Chapter
1602 Bellmore Avenue
North Bellmore NY 11710
(516) 783-3370

LFA, Marguerite Curri Chapter
P.O. Box 853
Utica NY 13503
(315) 732-4291

LFA, Northeastern New York
    Chapter
126 State Street
Albany NY 12207
(518) 465-3603

LFA, Rockland/Orange County
    Chapter
14 Kingston Drive
Spring Valley NY 10977
(914) 354-0372

LFA, Westchester Chapter
Munger Pavilion
Valhalla NY 10595
(914) 948-1032

LFA, Western New York Chapter
205 Yorkshire Road
Tonawanda NY 14150
(716) 835-7161

LFA, New York Southern Tier
    Chapter
19 Chanango Street, Suite 410
Binghamton NY 13901
(607) 772-6522 or
(800) 675-4546

S.L.E. Foundation
149 Madison Avenue
New York NY 10016
(212) 685-4118

## North Carolina

LFA, Charlotte Chapter
101 Colville Road
Charlotte NC 28207
(704) 375-8787

LFA, Raleigh Chapter
P.O. Box 10171
Raleigh NC 27605
(919) 821-0033

LFA, Western North Carolina
    Chapter
P.O. Box 9212
Asheville NC 28815
(704) 524-5200 or 649-3174

LFA, Winston-Triad Chapter
2841 Foxwood Lane
Winston-Salem NC 27103
(919) 768-1493

## Ohio

LFA, Akron Area Chapter
942 North Main Street, #23
Akron OH 44310
(216) 253-1717

LFA, Columbus Marcy Zitron
Chapter
5180 East Main Street
Columbus OH 43213
(614) 221-0811

LFA, Greater Cleveland Chapter
P.O. Box 6506
Cleveland OH 44101
(216) 531-6563

LFA, Northwest Ohio Chapter
1615 Washington Avenue
Findlay OH 45840
(419) 423-9313

LFA, Stark County Chapter
P.O. Box 1038
Massillon OH 44648
(216) 833-4811

## Oklahoma

Oklahoma Lupus Association
3131 North MacArthur, Suite 140D
Oklahoma City OK 73122
(405) 495-8787

## Pennsylvania

Lupus Alert
P.O. Box 8
Folsom PA 19033
(215) 532-6771

LFA, Delaware Valley Chapter
44 West Lancaster Avenue
Ardmore PA 19003
(215) 649-9202

LFA, Northeast Pennsylvania
Chapter
822 Ash Avenue
Scranton PA 18510
(717) 342-6146

LFA, Northwestern Pennsylvania
Chapter
P.O. Box 885
Erie PA 16512
(814) 866-0226

LFA, Western Pennsylvania
Chapter
1323 Forbes Avenue, Suite 200
Pittsburgh PA 15219
(412) 261-5886 or
(800) 800-5776

Lupus Foundation of Philadelphia
5415 Claridge Street
Philadelphia PA 19124
(215) 743-7171

Pennsylvania Lupus Foundation
P.O. Box 264
Wayne PA 19087
(215) 477-7020

## Rhode Island

LFA, Rhode Island Chapter
8 Fallon Avenue
Providence RI 02908
(401) 421-7227

## South Carolina

LFA, South Carolina Chapter
P.O. Box 7511
Columbia SC 29202
(803) 794-1000

## Tennessee

LFA, East Tennessee Chapter
5612 Kingston Pike, Suite 5
Knoxville TN 37919
(615) 584-5215

LFA, Memphis Area Chapter
3181 Poplar Avenue, Suite 100
Memphis TN 38111
(901) 324-8210 (hotline) or 458-5302

LFA, Nashville Area Chapter
2200 21st Avenue, Suite 253
Nashville TN 37212
(615) 298-2273

## Texas

LFA, El Paso Chapter
P.O. Box 4965
El Paso TX 79914
(915) 751-6941

LFA, North Texas Chapter
2997 LBJ Freeway, Suite 108N
Dallas TX 75234
(214) 484-0503 or
(800) 262-4944 (TX only)

LFA, Texas Gulf Coast Chapter
3100 Timmons Lane, #410
Houston TX 77027
(713) 623-8267 or
(800) 458-7870 (TX only)

LFA, Lubbock Area Chapter
4304 31st Street
Lubbock TX 79410
(806) 797-4239

San Antonio Lupus Foundation
McCullough Medical Center
4118 McCullough Avenue, #19
San Antonio TX 78212
(210) 824-1344

## Utah

LFA, Utah Chapter
4036 South 2700 East
Salt Lake City UT 84124
(801) 277-1767 or
(800) 657-6398

## Vermont

LFA, Vermont Chapter
P.O. Box 209
South Barre VT 05670
(802) 479-2326

## Virginia

LFA, Central Virginia Chapter
2720 Enterprise Parkway, Suite 104
Richmond VA 23294
(804) 262-9622

LFA, Eastern Virginia Chapter
Pembroke One
281 Independence Boulevard,
    Suite 442
Virginia Beach VA 23462
(804) 471-9715 (hotline) or 490-2793

## West Virginia

LFA, Kanawha Valley Chapter
P.O. Box 8274
South Charleston WV 25303
(304) 340-3517

## Wisconsin

Lupus Society of Wisconsin
3200 North Summit Avenue
Milwaukee WI 53211
(414) 781-1111

# Glossary

Note: Words and phrases in SMALL CAPITALS will be found in this glossary.

**acetylation**  a step in the metabolization of certain drugs; the rate at which this process takes place in a particular individual may determine whether or not a drug is likely to cause a lupus-like syndrome.

**acetyltransferase**  an enzyme involved in ACETYLATION.

**ACL**  the abbreviation for ANTI-CARDIOLIPIN antibody.

**ACTH**  adrenocorticotrophic hormone; a hormone, produced by the pituitary gland, that stimulates cortisol production by the adrenal glands.

**acyclovir**  an antiviral drug used in the treatment of certain herpes-virus infections.

**AFP**  the abbreviation for ALPHA-FETOPROTEIN.

231

**alopecia**   abnormal loss or absence of hair.

**alpha-fetoprotein**   a substance produced mainly by the fetal liver; assessment of levels in the maternal circulation may reveal information concerning fetal development.

**amenorrhea**   absence of menstruation.

**ANA**   the abbreviation for ANTINUCLEAR ANTIBODIES.

**androgens**   the sex-determinant hormones predominant in men.

**anemia**   a deficit in red blood cells.

**antibody**   a substance produced by the immune system in response to an infectious agent or other antigenic stimulus.

**anti-cardiolipin**   an ANTI-PHOSPHOLIPID antibody associated with a variety of circulatory problems and with difficulties and adverse outcomes in pregnancy.

**anticoagulant**   see LUPUS ANTICOAGULANT.

**antigen**   a protein that provokes ANTIBODY production by the immune system.

**antigen-antibody complexes**   units of bound-together ANTIGEN and ANTIBODY, typically producing inflammation.

**anti-inflammatory drugs**   drugs designed specifically to diminish inflammation.

**antimalarials**   a class of drugs originally developed to treat malaria which have been found helpful in the treatment of lupus.

**antinuclear antibodies**   ANTIBODIES that act against material from cell nuclei (cores).

**anti-phospholipids**   ANTIBODIES directed against substances in cell membranes; they include ANTI-CARDIOLIPIN and LUPUS ANTICOAGULANT.

**APLs**   the abbreviation for ANTI-PHOSPHOLIPIDS.

**arteriole**   a tiny branch of an artery.

**arthralgia**   pain in a joint or joints.

**arthritis**   inflammation of a joint or joints.

**arthropathy**  joint disease.

**arthroplasty**  joint surgery.

**autoantibodies**  ANTIBODIES that act against the body's own tissues.

**autoimmune disorder (or disease)**  a condition characterized by the production of AUTOANTIBODIES.

**avascular necrosis**  NECROSIS due to diminished blood supply.

**azathioprine**  an anti-cancer drug also sometimes used as an IMMUNOSUPPRESSANT.

**baseline values**  numbers, such as those obtained from initial blood or urine tests, used for comparison with later ones.

**B-cells**  a subclass of LYMPHOCYTES that produce ANTIBODIES.

**biopsy**  removal of a small sample of tissue for microscopic examination.

**biphosphonates**  a class of drugs useful, or potentially useful, in the treatment of OSTEOPOROSIS.

**bromocriptine**  a drug inhibiting the release of PROLACTIN, a pituitary hormone.

**BUN**  the abbreviation for blood urea nitrogen, the proportion of nitrogen in a blood sample deriving from its UREA content; an elevated value may hint of kidney dysfunction.

**calcitonin**  a thyroid hormone essential to the bone REMODELING process.

**calcitriol**  the active form of vitamin D.

**cancellous bone**  TRABECULAR BONE.

**cardiolipin**  a PHOSPHOLIPID found in cells lining blood vessels; formerly called "heart antigen."

**casts**  see CELLULAR CASTS.

**CBC**  the abbreviation for COMPLETE BLOOD COUNT.

**cellular casts**  fragments of bodily substances such as HEMOGLOBIN; their presence in urine may suggest kidney disease.

**chloroquines**   a class of antimalarial drugs also used in the treatment of lupus.

**collagen**   a protein substance that is a major component of connective tissue in the joints and elsewhere.

**collagen disease**   formerly, a term used to refer to lupus and other systemic rheumatic AUTOIMMUNE DISORDERS, now known as connective-tissue diseases.

**compact bone**   CORTICAL BONE.

**complement system**   a component of the immune system, consisting of a series of proteins that perform various actions in support of ANTIBODY activity.

**complete blood count**   analysis of the number of cells—ERYTHROCYTES, LEUKOCYTES, and THROMBOCYTES—in a quantity of blood.

**concordant**   having a particular characteristic in common; persons are said to be "concordant for" the trait in question.

**congenital**   present at birth.

**core decompression**   a surgical procedure for the treatment of OSTEONECROSIS.

**cortical bone**   a type of bone found primarily in the long bones of the arms and legs and constituting approximately 80 percent of the skeleton.

**corticosteroid**   any of a number of medications resembling cortisol, a hormone produced by the cortex (outer layer) of the adrenal glands; their effect is to inhibit inflammatory processes.

**creatinine**   a waste product of muscle activity, normally excreted in the urine; the creatinine clearance rate is a measure of kidney function.

**cutaneous**   relating to the skin.

**cyclophosphamide**   an anti-cancer drug (cytotoxic agent) also used as an IMMUNOSUPPRESSANT in the treatment of lupus.

**cyclosporin**   an IMMUNOSUPPRESSANT drug used in transplant surgery and, to a limited degree, experimentally to treat lupus.

**danazol**   a synthetic ANDROGEN derivative.

**densitometry**   the measurement of bone density, used in the detection of OSTEOPOROSIS.

**dexamethasone**   a CORTICOSTEROID.

**dialysis**   see HEMODIALYSIS.

**discoid lupus (discoid lupus erythematosus; DLE)**   lupus limited to the skin, characterized by thick, reddish, roughly disk-shaped lesions; formerly considered a separate disease.

**discordant**   differing as to a particular characteristic; the opposite of CONCORDANT.

**dizygotic**   originating from two different fertilized egg cells; dizygotic twins are fraternal (nonidentical) twins.

**DNA**   deoxyribonucleic acid, a component of cell nuclei and the substance of the genes that transmit hereditary information.

**dorsal kyphosis**   a convex curvature of the spine caused by vertebral compression fracture due to OSTEOPOROSIS; "dowager's hump."

**edema**   swelling associated with fluid retention.

**emboli**   migrating fragments of blood clots.

**ENA**   the abbreviation for EXTRACTABLE NUCLEAR ANTIGEN.

**end stage**   in reference to renal disease, denoting that point at which kidney impairment has become potentially life-threatening.

**endocarditis**   see LIBMAN-SACKS ENDOCARDITIS.

**endorphins**   substances, produced by the brain, that bind to opiate receptors and raise the pain threshold; coined from "endogenous morphine." (Opiates are a broad class of drugs including natural derivatives of opium, such as morphine, as well as many synthetics used chiefly to treat severe pain.)

**erythema nodosum**   a form of VASCULITIS characterized by painful reddish nodules; it may be secondary to a number of infections and may also occur in reaction to various drugs.

**erythrocyte**   red cell, a type of blood cell.

**erythrocyte sedimentation rate**   the sinking velocity of red cells within a quantity of drawn blood; it may be elevated in a number of AUTOIMMUNE and other conditions.

**ESR**   the abbreviation for ERYTHROCYTE SEDIMENTATION RATE.

**estrogens**   the sex-determinant hormones predominant in women.

**etidronate**   a drug for treatment of OSTEOPOROSIS.

**extractable nuclear antigen**   any of a number of specific ANTIGENS, found within the nuclei (inner cores) of cells, to which a significant proportion of persons with lupus—and certain other disorders—have demonstrated ANTIBODIES.

**false-positive**   in reference to testing, erroneously suggesting the presence of a disease or other characteristic.

**first-degree relative**   a biological parent, child, or sibling.

**flare**   in lupus, a period of increased disease activity.

**glomeruli**   the tufts comprising the kidney's filtering apparatus.

**glomerulonephritis**   kidney inflammation involving the GLOMERULI.

**glucocorticoid**   CORTICOSTEROID.

**graft**   a transplanted organ.

**heart block**   a condition involving heartbeat irregularities due to misfiring of certain electrical signals within the heart.

**hematologic**   relating to the blood.

**hematuria**   a condition in which the urine contains red blood cells.

**hemodialysis**   filtering of the blood through a mechanical device outside the body to remove waste materials.

**hemoglobin**   the oxygen-transporting pigment of the blood; it is found in the ERYTHROCYTES.

**hemolytic anemia**   ANEMIA due to abnormally rapid destruction of red blood cells.

**herpes zoster**   shingles.

**histocompatibility**   compatibility of tissues, as between an organ donor and recipient.

**HLA system**   a region, found on the sixth human chromosome, controlling a number of immunologic responses. The letters stand for "human leukocyte antigen."

**hydroxychloroquine**   one of the antimalarial drugs used to treat lupus.

**immune complexes**   see ANTIGEN-ANTIBODY COMPLEXES.

**immune globulin**   a substance, derived from human plasma, containing ANTIBODIES to a particular infectious agent; it is used to provide temporary "passive immunization."

**immunoglobulins**   substances, produced by B-CELLS, containing ANTIGEN-specific ANTIBODIES.

**immunologic**   pertaining to the body's immune-defense system.

**immunosuppressants**   agents employed to suppress the immune system (e.g., in organ transplantation and in autoimmune disease) and to treat malignancies.

**ischemic**   characterized by localized ANEMIA due to obstruction of blood supply.

**ITP**   the abbreviation for immune THROMBOCYTOPENIA—a platelet deficit caused by autoimmune activity.

**keratoconjunctivitis sicca**   SJÖGREN'S SYNDROME specifically involving the tear glands and accompanied by inflammation of the mucous membranes of the eye.

**kyphosis**   see DORSAL KYPHOSIS.

**LAC**   the abbreviation for LUPUS ANTICOAGULANT.

**latex fixation test**   a test for RHEUMATOID FACTOR.

**LE cell**   a unique leukocyte showing evidence of aberrant PHAGOCYTOSIS; a positive LE-cell test is among the diagnostic criteria for lupus.

**LE prep**   LE-cell test.

**lesion**   any more or less circumscribed structural change due to injury or disease; often, but not necessarily, used in reference to the skin.

**leukocyte**   white cell, a type of blood cell.

**leukopenia**   a deficit in white blood cells.

**Libman-Sacks endocarditis**   a condition characterized by wart-like growths on the heart valves.

**lupus anticoagulant**   an ANTI-PHOSPHOLIPID ANTIBODY associated with a tendency to clot formation and with pregnancy loss.

**lupus tuberculosis, lupus vulgaris**   obsolete terms for cutaneous tuberculosis involving the face.

**lymphadenopathy**   enlarged lymph nodes; "swollen glands."

**lymphocyte**   a type of white blood cell especially active in the immune system.

**lymphokines**   infection-fighting substances produced by T-CELLS.

**lymphopenia**   a deficit in LYMPHOCYTES.

**magnetic resonance imaging**   a noninvasive diagnostic technique using radiofrequency pulses, permitting three-dimensional visualization of various body tissues.

**mammography**   X ray of the breast.

**menopause**   the cessation of menstruation; the constellation of hormonal and other changes occurring at this time of life, often referred to as "menopause," is properly termed the climacteric.

**methylprednisolone**   a CORTICOSTEROID.

**MHC**   an alternate designation for HLA. The letters stand for "major histocompatibility complex."

**monoclonal antibodies**   ANTIBODIES derived from a single cell, created and administered for experimental therapeutic purposes.

**monozygotic**   originating from the same fertilized egg cell; monozygotic twins are genetically identical.

**MRI**   the abbreviation for MAGNETIC RESONANCE IMAGING.

**mycoplasmas**   a class of infectious organisms (they are neither bacteria nor viruses) linked to a variety of conditions and recently explored in connection with lupus.

**myositis**   muscle inflammation.

**necrosis**   deterioration or erosion—e.g., of bone.

**negative**   in reference to laboratory testing or other diagnostic procedures, unremarkable; displaying no departure from normal, no presence of microorganisms, etc.

**"neonatal lupus"**   a newborn syndrome characterized chiefly by a transient rash and transient blood-test abnormalities.

**nephritis**   kidney inflammation.

**nephrosis, nephrotic syndrome**   degenerative kidney disease.

**nifedipine**   a drug used to treat coronary heart disease which has also been found helpful in RAYNAUD'S PHENOMENON.

**NSAID**   a commonly employed acronym for "nonsteroidal anti-inflammatory drug"; it is pronounced "EN-sade."

**organic murmur**   a heart sound signaling a structural aberration.

**osteoblasts and osteoclasts**   cells involved in the process of bone REMODELING.

**osteonecrosis**   NECROSIS of bone.

**osteoporosis**   a state of skeletal fragility, which may be due to hormone or mineral deficiency or may be induced by certain drugs.

**oxalates**   chemicals, found in certain foods, that lower the level of calcium absorption.

**partial thromboplastin time**   a test for the presence of LUPUS ANTICO-AGULANT.

**pericarditis**   inflammation of the pericardium, the outer membrane surrounding the heart.

**peripheral joints**   those of the hands, arms, feet, and legs.

**petechiae**   small purplish-red "bruises" that are evidence of tiny hemorrhages within the skin.

**phagocytosis**   the process of ingestion—by certain white cells known as phagocytes—of bacteria, cellular debris, foreign material, etc.

**pheresis**   see PLASMAPHERESIS.

**phlebitis**   venous inflammation.

**phospholipids**   substances, found universally in cell membranes, that may stimulate the production of ANTIBODIES.

**photosensitive**   abnormally reactive to light, especially ultraviolet light.

**plasma**   the fluid in which the blood cells are suspended.

**plasmapheresis**   the removal of a quantity of blood PLASMA and its replacement by an inert solution in order to reduce the quantity of circulating ANTIBODIES, etc.

**platelet**   THROMBOCYTE.

**pleurisy** or **pleuritis**   inflammation of the pleura, the membrane lining the chest cavity.

**polyarthritis**   simultaneous inflammation of a number of joints.

**positive**   in reference to laboratory testing or other diagnostic procedures, indicating the presence of microorganisms, departure from normal values, etc.

**prednisolone, prednisone**   two of the CORTICOSTEROIDS.

**preeclampsia**   a complication of pregnancy, posing a serious threat to mother and child, characterized by heightened blood pressure and EDEMA.

**progesterone**   a hormone, produced by the ovaries and the placenta, essential to sustaining pregnancy.

**prolactin**   a pituitary hormone that stimulates breast enlargement and milk production (lactation); lactogenic hormone.

**proteinuria**   the abnormal presence of certain proteins in the urine.

**psoralens**   chemical constituents of certain plants which, if ingested or applied to the skin, can heighten PHOTOSENSITIVITY.

**PTT**   the abbreviation for PARTIAL THROMBOPLASTIN TIME.

**pulmonary**   relating to the lungs.

**pulse therapy** the administration of relatively high doses of a drug by intravenous injection at specific intervals.

**pyrexia** fever.

**Raynaud's phenomenon** abnormal paling and numbing of the fingers or toes, in reaction to cold or other stimuli, due to VASOSPASM.

**remission** a period of abatement of signs and symptoms of a disease.

**remodeling** the cyclic process of bone resorption and rebuilding.

**renal** relating to the kidneys.

**rheumatoid factor** an ANTIBODY found in rheumatoid arthritis and in some patients with other autoimmune disorders.

**rheumatology** the branch of medicine focusing on lupus, rheumatoid arthritis, and other AUTOIMMUNE and arthritic disorders; it is a subspecialty of internal medicine.

**salicylates** a family of ANTI-INFLAMMATORY DRUGS, including aspirin and others.

**"sed rate"** ERYTHROCYTE SEDIMENTATION RATE.

**sensitivity** in reference to diagnostic screening tests, the relative proportion of cases of a disease or other condition likely to be recognized.

**sicca syndrome** SJÖGREN'S SYNDROME.

**Sjögren's syndrome** a condition involving dysfunction of various moisture-producing glands, prominently those producing saliva and tears.

**specificity** in reference to diagnostic screening tests, the ability to distinguish a disease or condition from others.

**splenectomy** surgical removal of the spleen.

**spontaneous abortion** miscarriage.

**steroid** in the context of this book, short for CORTICOSTEROID.

**subacute bacterial endocarditis** an infection of the heart lesions in LIBMAN-SACKS ENDOCARDITIS.

**systemic**   affecting the body as a whole; not localized to one area, organ, or type of tissue.

**systemic lupus erythematosus**   the full medical name of the disease generally referred to simply as lupus. See page 6.

**T-cells**   a subclass of LYMPHOCYTES.

**thrombocyte**   clotting cell, a type of blood cell.

**thrombocytopenia**   a deficit of THROMBOCYTES.

**thrombophlebitis**   PHLEBITIS involving clot formation.

**thrombosis**   clot formation within a blood vessel.

**TLI**   the abbreviation for TOTAL LYMPHOID IRRADIATION.

**total lymphoid irradiation**   the irradiation of lymph nodes and other tissues in order to suppress ANTIBODY production.

**toxemia of pregnancy**   PREECLAMPSIA.

**trabecular bone**   bone with a lattice-like structure, characteristic of the spine.

**Tripterygium**   a genus of Asian plants, extracts of which have been used there, and are being explored elsewhere, to treat AUTOIMMUNE disease.

**urea**   a metabolic end-product that is a normal component of urine.

**uremia**   an excess of waste materials, normally eliminated by the kidneys, in the blood.

**varicella**   chickenpox.

**varicella-zoster virus (VZV)**   the herpesvirus that causes chicken-pox and shingles.

**vasculitis**   blood-vessel inflammation.

**vasospasm**   spasmodic occlusion of small blood vessels.

**verrucous endocarditis**   LIBMAN-SACKS ENDOCARDITIS.

**VZIG**   VARICELLA-ZOSTER IMMUNE GLOBULIN.

**xerostomia**   dryness of the mouth.

# Selected Bibliography

## Introduction

"Doctors Treat More Lupus Than National Statistics Indicate." *Medical World News*, January 1991, p. 31.

Dafna D. Gladman. "Prognosis of Systemic Lupus Erythematosus and Factors That Affect It." *Current Opinion in Rheumatology* 1992; 4:681-87.

## Chapter 2

Maria H. Esteva et al. "False Positive Results for Antibody to HIV in Two Men with Systemic Lupus Erythematosus." *Annals of the Rheumatic Diseases* 1992; 51:1071-73.

R. Jindal et al. "False Positive Tests for HIV in a Woman with Lupus and Renal Failure" (letter). *The New England Journal of Medicine* 1993; 328:1281-82.

## Chapter 3

Frank C. Arnett. "Genetic Factors and Lupus." *Lupus News* (Lupus Foundation of America) 1992; Vol. 12, No. 1, p. 4.

Michael McDermott and Hugh McDevitt. "The Immunogenetics of Rheumatic Diseases." *Bulletin On the Rheumatic Diseases* (Arthritis Foundation) 1989; Vol. 38, No. 1, pp. 1-10.

John D. Reveille. "The Molecular Genetics of Systemic Lupus Erythematosus and Sjögren's Syndrome." *Current Opinion in Rheumatology* 1992; 4:644-56.

Denny L. Tuffanelli. "What Is the Magnitude of the Problem of Lupus Erythematosus?" *Lupus News* 1991; Vol. 11, No. 2, pp. 1-2.

Mikhail Folomeev, Maxime Dougados, et al. "Plasma Sex Hormones and Aromatase Activity in Tissues of Patients with Systemic Lupus Erythematosus." *Lupus* 1992; 1:191-95.

Josep Font, Ricard Cervera, et al. "Systemic Lupus Erythematosus in Men: Clinical and Immunological Characteristics." *Annals of the Rheumatic Diseases* 1992; 51:1050-52.

A. Olcay Aydintug, Ines Domenech, et al. "Systemic Lupus Erythematosus in Males: Analysis of Clinical and Laboratory Features." *Lupus* 1992; 1:295-98.

A. Hoffmann, S.J. Albig, et al. "Active Human Herpesvirus Type 6 Infection in Patients with SLE, RA, and Fibromyalgia." *Lupus* 1992; 1(supp):172.

Norman Talal. "Lupus and a Retrovirus: A Medical Detective Story." *Lupus News* 1992; Vol. 12, No. 2, p. 6.

C. Jorgensen, P. Corbeau, et al. "Detection of Serum Antibodies to Core Proteins of $HIV_1$ in Lymphopenic Systemic Lupus Erythematosus." *Lupus* 1992; 1(supp):186.

Alfred D. Steinberg, moderator, et al. "Systemic Lupus Erythematosus" (edited summary of NIH conference). *Annals of Internal Medicine* 1991; 115:548-59.

"'Superantigens' May Play Etiologic Role in SLE, RA." *Rheumatology News*, May 1990; pp. 1, 10.

K.S. Ginsburg et al. "Mycoplasma Ureaplasma Urealyticum and Mycoplasma Hominis in Women with Systemic Lupus Erythematosus." *Lupus* 1992; 1(supp):172.

D.R.E. Jones et al. "Autoantibodies in Pet Dogs Owned by Patients with Systemic Lupus Erythematosus." *The Lancet* 1992; 339:1378-80.

**Chapter 5**

John M. Esdaile. "Antimalarials in SLE." *Lupus News* 1992; Vol. 12, No. 1, pp. 1-3.

The Canadian Hydroxychloroquine Study Group. "A Randomized Study of the Effect of Withdrawing Hydroxychloroquine Sulfate in Systemic Lupus Erythematosus." *The New England Journal of Medicine* 1991; 324:150-54.

Michelle Petri et al. "Side Effects of Medications Prescribed for Systemic Lupus Erythematosus." *Arthritis & Rheumatism* 1992; 35:S358.

Yehuda Shoenfeld and Donato Alarcon-Segovia. "The Mosaic of Systemic Lupus Erythematosus: Highlights of the Third International Conference on SLE 13-15 April 1992." *Lupus* 1992; 1:269-83.

D.J. Wallace. "A New Role for Hydroxychloroquine in the 1990s?" *Lupus* 1992; 1(supp):98.

Michelle Petri et al. "The Effect of Prednisone and Hydroxychloroquine on Coronary Artery Disease Risk Factors in SLE." *Arthritis & Rheumatism* 1992; 35:S54.

"Adding Cyclophosphamide to Prednisone Spares Renal Function in Lupus Nephritis." *Today in Medicine / Musculoskeletal Medicine*, November/December 1991; p. 9.

J.E. Balow, D. Boumpas, et al. "Severe Lupus Nephritis: Controlled Trial of Pulse Methylprednisolone versus Cyclophosphamide." *Lupus* 1992; 1(supp):88.

P. Langevitz et al. "Cyclophosphamide Pulse Therapy in Lupus Nephritis." *Lupus* 1992; 1(supp):112.

Le Thi Huong Du, Jean-Charles Piette, et al. "Efficacy and Limits of Intravenous Cyclophosphamide in Systemic Lupus Erythematosus." *Lupus* 1992; 1(supp):112.

Sahar M. Dawisha, Cheryl Yarboro, et al. "Monthly Oral Bolus Cyclophosphamide Therapy in Systemic Lupus Erythematosus." *Arthritis & Rheumatism* 1992; 35:S153.

Frederick W. Willer and Lori A. Love. "Prevention of Predictable Raynaud's Phenomenon by Sublingual Nifedipine" (letter). *The New England Journal of Medicine* 1987; 317:1476.

**Chapter 6**

Masayuki Yasuda et al. "Corticosteroid-Induced Glaucoma Complication in Patients with Systemic Lupus Erythematosus." *Lupus* 1992; 1(supp):171.

**Chapter 7**

M. Abeles et al. "The Association of Osteonecrosis in SLE with Anticardiolipin Antibodies." *Lupus* 1992; 1(supp):47.

Michelle Petri et al. "Risk Factors for Avascular Necrosis in SLE." *Arthritis & Rheumatism* 1992; 35:S110.

Dafna D. Gladman. "Prognosis of Systemic Lupus Erythematosus and the Factors That Affect It." *Current Opinion in Rheumatology* 1991; 3:789-96.

Steve Takemoto, Paul I. Terasaki, et al. for the UNOS Scientific Renal Transplant Registry. "Survival of Nationally Shared, HLA-Matched Kidney Transplants from Cadaveric Donors." *The New England Journal of Medicine* 1992; 327:834-39.

## Chapter 8

Michelle Petri, Daniel Goldman, et al. "Prevalence of and Factors Associated with Fractures in SLE." *Arthritis & Rheumatism* 1992; 35:S109.

Murray W. Tilyard et al. "Treatment of Postmenopausal Osteoporosis with Calcitriol or Calcium." *The New England Journal of Medicine* 1992; 326:357-62.

B. Lawrence Riggs and L. Joseph Melton III. "The Prevention and Treatment of Osteoporosis." *The New England Journal of Medicine* 1992; 327:620-27.

"Etidronate for Postmenopausal Osteoporosis." *The Medical Letter* 1990; 32:111-12.

"Choice of Drugs for Postmenopausal Osteoporosis." *The Medical Letter* 1992; 34:101-02.

Belinda Lees, Theya Molleson, et al. "Differences in Proximal Femur Bone Density over Two Centuries." *The Lancet* 1993; 341:673-75.

## Chapter 9

Michelle Petri et al. "Risk Factors for Preterm Birth in Lupus Pregnancy." *Lupus* 1992; 1(supp):159.

Yehuda Shoenfeld and Margalit Lorber. "Animal Models of SLE and Anti-Phospholipid Syndrome Demonstrate the Role of Autoantibodies in Causing Disease." *Lupus News* 1992; Vol. 12, No. 3, pp. 1-2.

Michelle Petri, Audrey Chan, et al. "Maternal Alphafetoprotein in Lupus Pregnancy." *Arthritis & Rheumatism* 1992; 35:S108.

S. Schwartzman et al. "Use of Low Dose Steroids in the Prevention of Fetal Loss in Women with Antiphospholipid Antibodies." *Arthritis & Rheumatism* 1992; 35:S153.

A. Mathieu, G.D. Sebastiani, et al. "Obstetric and Gynecological Manifestations in Systemic Lupus Erythematosus." *Lupus* 1992; 1(supp):57.

Jill P. Buyon. "Systemic Lupus Erythematosus and Pregnancy." *Cliniguide to Rheumatology* 1991; Vol. 1, No. 4, pp. 1-8.

Jonathan Waltuck and Jill P. Buyon. "Neonatal and Maternal Outcome in Complete Heart Block." *Arthritis & Rheumatism* 1992; 35:S60.

**Chapter 10**

Evelyn V. Hess and Anne-Barbara Mongey. "Drug-Related Lupus." *Bulletin on the Rheumatic Diseases* 1991; Vol. 40, No. 4, pp. 1-8.

"Lovastatin-Induced Lupus." *Physicians' Drug Alert* 1991; XII: 73-74.

Michael McDermott and Hugh McDevitt. "The Immunogenetics of Rheumatic Diseases." *Bulletin on the Rheumatic Diseases* 1989, Vol. 38, No. 1, pp. 1-10.

Bruce Freundlich et al. "A Sjögren's-Like Syndrome in Women with Silicone-Gel Breast Implants." *Arthritis & Rheumatism* 1992; 35:S67.

Frank B. Vasey, Deborah Havice, et al. "Clinical Manifestations of Fifty Consecutive Women with Silicone Breast Implants and Connective Tissue Disease." *Arthritis & Rheumatism* 1992; 35:S212.

Steven R. Weiner et al. "Chronic Arthropathy after Silicone Augmentation Mammoplasty." *Arthritis & Rheumatism* 1992; 35:S212.

"Two Studies Yield New Data on Breast Implants." *FDA Consumer*, June 1993; pp. 3-4.

Neal Handel, Melvin J. Silverstein, et al. "Factors Affecting Mammographic Visualization of the Breast after Augmentation Mammoplasty." *Journal of the American Medical Association* 1992; 268:1913-17.

Betty Rollin. "The Saline Solution." *New York Times*, February 23, 1992; p. E15.

**Chapter 11**

L. Domenech, P. Valdivielso, et al. "Dyslipoproteinemia Induced by Steroids in Systemic Lupus Erythematosus." *Lupus* 1992; 1(supp):52.

E.A. Kitsis, H.M. Belmont, et al. "Cardiac Risk Factors in Patients with Systemic Lupus Erythematosus." *Arthritis & Rheumatism* 1992; 35:S108.

Jeffrey P. Callen et al. "Photoexacerbation of Cutaneous Lupus Erythematosus Due to UVA Emissions from a Photocopier." *Arthritis & Rheumatism* 1992; 35:S357.

"Choice of Drugs for Postmenopausal Osteoporosis." *The Medical Letter* 1992; 34:101-02.

Kathryn North and Llewelyn Davies. "Postexercise Headache in Menopausal Women [Receiving Transdermal Estrogen]" (letter). *The Lancet* 1993; 341:972.

**Chapter 12**

Randolph C. Byrd. "Positive Therapeutic Effects of Intercessory Prayer in a Coronary Care Unit Population." *Southern Medical Journal* 1988; 81:826-29.

## Chapter 14

Edmund J. Lewis, Lawrence G. Hunsicker, et al. "A Controlled Trial of Plasmapheresis Therapy in Severe Lupus Nephritis." *The New England Journal of Medicine* 1992; 326:1373-79.

Hans H. Euler et al. "Plasmapheresis for Lupus Nephritis" (letters in reaction to the above, with a response from the authors). *The New England Journal of Medicine* 1992; 327:1028-30.

Hans H. Euler et al. "Treatment-Free Remission Following Plasmapheresis and Subsequent Pulse Cyclophosphamide in Severe SLE." *Arthritis & Rheumatism* 1992; 35:S35.

M. Hochfeld, M. Druzin, et al. "Preservation of Ovarian Function in Patients with Lupus Nephritis: Cyclophosphamide versus Total Lymphoid Irradiation." *Arthritis & Rheumatism* 1992; 35:S208.

John H. Klippel et al. "New Therapies for the Rheumatic Diseases." *Bulletin on the Rheumatic Diseases* 1989; Vol. 38, No. 4, pp. 1-8.

Falk Hiepe, Bernhard Thiele, et al. "Treatment of Severe Systemic Lupus Erythematosus with an Anti-CD4 Monoclonal Antibody." *Arthritis & Rheumatism* 1992; 35:S55.

Bernhard Thiele, Falk Hiepe, et al. "Investigation of the Kinetic of CD4+ Cells during Therapy with Anti-CD4 Antibody in Lupus Patients." *Arthritis & Rheumatism* 1992; 35:S153.

F. Hiepe, H.-D. Volk, et al. "Treatment of Severe Systemic Lupus Erythematosus with an Anti-CD4 Monoclonal Antibody." *Lupus* 1992; 1(supp):48.

Ronald F. van Vollenhoven and Hugh O. McDevitt. "Studies of the Treatment of Nephritis in NZB/NZW Mice with Dehydroepiandrosterone." *Arthritis & Rheumatism* 1992; 35:S207.

Ronald F. van Vollenhoven, Lynda Lee, et al. "Treatment of Systemic Lupus Erythematosus with Dehydroepiandrosterone." *Arthritis & Rheumatism* 1992; 35:S55.

Feng Shufang et al. "Danazol for SLE." *Lupus* 1992; 1(supp):50.

Z. Sthoeger et al. "The Beneficial Effect of Estrogen Antagonists in Experimental Lupus Erythematosus." *Lupus* 1992; 1(supp):19.

John D. Mountz and Carl K. Edwards III. "Murine Models of Autoimmune Disease." *Current Opinion in Rheumatology* 1992; 4:621-29.

Yehuda Shoenfeld and Donato Alarcon-Segovia. "The Mosaic of Systemic Lupus Erythematosus: Highlights of the Third International Conference on SLE 13-15 April 1992." *Lupus* 1992; 1:269-83.

Qin Wan-zhang. "Study of Extract of Tripterygium Wilfordii in Treatment of 206 Patients with Systemic Lupus Erythematosus." *Lupus* 1992; 1(supp):169.

Wen-Zhen Gu, Subhashis Banerjee, et al. "Suppression of Renal Disease and Arthritis and Prolongation of Survival in MRL Mice Treated with an Extract of Tripterygium Wilfordii." *Arthritis & Rheumatism* 1992; 35:S207.

Fulin Tang et al. "Effect of 'T2,' a Chinese Herbal Medication, on Lymphocyte Functions in Systemic Lupus Erythematosus." *Arthritis & Rheumatism* 1992; 35:S359.

R. Bambauer et al. "Nephrotoxicity of Cyclosporin A in the Treatment of Systemic Lupus Erythematosus." *Lupus* 1992; 1(supp):109.

O. Matsumura et al. "Therapeutic Effect of Cyclosporin in SLE." *Lupus* 1992; 1(supp):110.

R. Bambauer et al. "Cyclosporin A in Systemic Lupus Erythematosus." *Lupus* 1992; 1(supp):169.

# Index

ACE (angiotensin-converting-
enzyme) inhibitors, 140
Acetylation, acetyltransferase,
153-54
ACL, 95, 135-36, 174
ACTH, 90
Acyclovir, 98, 99, 206
Advil, 78
African-Americans, 42
Age at onset, 3, 43
in children, 198
AIDS, 1, 48-49, 50
false-positive test for, 34
Alcohol
and osteoporosis, 111
and pregnancy, 138

Alfalfa, 155, 166
Allergies, 13, 173, 174
to medications, 84
Alpha-fetoprotein (AFP), 139-40
Alternative therapies, 192-94
American Academy of Allergy
and Immunology, 160
American Academy of
Orthopaedic Surgeons
(AAOS), 119, 120
American Academy of Pediat-
rics, 202
American Board of Internal
Medicine, 60
American College of Radiology,
162

American College of Rheumatology (ACR), 3, 20, 107, 147, 157, 166, 172, 214, 216, 217
diagnostic criteria, 22-30, 200
Amines, 166
ANA, 29-30, 35, 39, 136
in drug-induced lupus, 151
Anemia, 26, 93-94
Animal research, 44, 136, 154, 168, 215, 216
Animals
and autoimmune disease, 55-57
and other human disease, 52
therapeutic role of, 193
"Anita," 10, 25-26
Ankylosing spondylitis, 40-41
Antacids, 79, 115
Anti-cardiolipin antibody. See ACL
Anti-phospholipid antibodies, 32-33, 41, 135-37, 141
Antibiotics, 54, 175
Antibodies, 29-30
anti-DNA, 28, 151
anti-ENA, 31-32, 151, 174
anti-La, 32, 41, 146, 147, 151, 176
antinuclear (ANA), 29-30, 35, 39, 151
anti-phospholipid, 32-33, 41, 135-37, 141, 174
anti-Ro, 32, 41, 146, 147, 151, 176
anti-Sm, 28, 41, 151
to histone, 151
monoclonal, 214-15

to viruses, 46-47, 49
Anticoagulant. See Lupus anticoagulant
Antigen-antibody complexes, 100
Antigens, 29-30
nuclear, 31-32
"super," 50
Antimalarials, 75-78
in pregnancy and breast-feeding, 143-45
Antinuclear antibodies. See ANA
APLs. See Anti-phospholipid antibodies
Apresoline, 152
Aralen, 75
Arthritis, 12-13, 16, 24-25, 32, 199
in women vs. men, 45
See also Rheumatoid arthritis
Arthritis Foundation, 61, 191, 193, 221
Arthroplasty, 97
Aseptic necrosis of bone. See Osteonecrosis
Asians, 42
Aspirin, 78, 79
in children, 204
and pregnancy, 141
Atabrine, 75
Autoimmunity, 2, 30. See also: Animals; Breast implants
Avascular necrosis of bone. See Osteonecrosis
Azathioprine, 81

B-cells, 48, 50, 80
Biopsy, kidney, 101-2
Biphosphonates, 117

Birth control pills. *See* Oral
contraceptives
Bleeding. *See* Hemorrhage
Blood pressure. *See* Hypertension
Blood urea nitrogen, 100
Board certification, 60
Bone structure, remodeling, 109-
10. *See also* Osteonecrosis;
Osteoporosis
Breast implants, 155-63, 166-67
Breast-feeding
and calcium, 112
and medications, 144-45
Bromocriptine, 216
BUN, 100
Bush, George and Barbara, 55
Butterfly rash, 7, 10, 22-23, 45, 199

Calcitonin, 109, 116
Calcitriol, 109, 111, 114, 115
Calcium, 109, 110, 111-15
Calcium channel blockers, 83
Calcium Information Center, 115
Canine lupus, 55
Cardiolipin. *See* ACL
Causes of lupus, theories on, 37-
57
Cazenave, Pierre, 7
Cellular casts, 26
Centers for Disease Control and
Prevention (CDC), 2, 178-79,
202, 205
Cervical cap, 148
Chickenpox, 53, 92, 98, 99, 204-7
Children, 43, 197-209
neonatal lupus, 146-47

Chloroquine, 75, 76, 77
Chloroquines. *See* Antimalarials
Chlorpromazine, 152
Cholesterol, 78, 169-70
drugs to lower, 152-53
Cimetidine, 79
Clinoril, 80
Collagen disease, 11, 12
Complement, 33
Complete blood count, 26-27
Compression fractures, 108
Condoms, 148
Congenital heart block, 146-47
Connective-tissue diseases,
disorders, 12, 20
"Connie," 10-12, 65-66, 69, 185,
188
Contraception, 147-48
Core decompression, 96-97
Corticosteroids, 85-92
in children, 202
combined, compared with
immunosuppressants, 81
and osteonecrosis, 95
and osteoporosis, 107,
110-11
in pregnancy and breast-
feeding, 143-45
and sexual activity, 180
and shingles, 98
Cosmetics, 166, 173-74
Counseling, 191-92
for children and teens, 208-9
Creatinine clearance rate, 100
Criteria, diagnostic, 22-30
Cyclophosphamide (Cytoxan),
81, 101

Danazol, 215
Dawson's encephalitis, 51-52
Densitometry, 108
Dental care, 174-75, 176-77
Diabetes mellitus, 2, 39, 41
Diagnosis, 4-5, 19-35
  in children, 200
Dialysis, 102
Diaphragm (contraceptive), 148
Didronel, 116-17
Diet, 167-70, 172
Dietary supplements, 169. *See
  also* Calcium
Disalcid, 79
Discoid lesions, 2, 23, 45, 199
DNA, 31
  antibodies to, 28, 151
  viruses, 46
Doctor. *See* Physician
Dorsal kyphosis, 108
Dow Corning, 157-58, 160
"Dowager's hump," 108
DQ, DR markers. *See* HLA
Drug-induced lupus, 149-54
Drugs. *See* Medications
Dryness (mouth, eyes, et al.), 15

"Eileen," 12-13, 27, 32, 71-72,
  86-88, 89, 185-86, 188-89, 190
Electroencephalogram (EEG), 26
ELISA, 34
"Elizabeth," 13-14, 27, 71, 76, 77,
  89, 94, 167, 185, 186-87, 190,
  195
Emotional factors, 69-72
  in children and teens, 207-9

End-stage renal disease, 102-5
Endocarditis. *See* Libman-Sacks
  endocarditis
Endorphins, 190-91
Environmental agents and lupus,
  54-57
Erythema infectiosum, 35
Erythema nodosum, 11
Erythrocyte sedimentation rate
  (ESR), 31
Estrogens, 43-44
  and osteoporosis, 110, 182-83
Etidronate, 116-17
Exercise, 118-31, 182-83, 189-91
Extractable nuclear antigens,
  31-32
Eyes, antimalarial effects on,
  76-77
Eyes, dry. *See* Sjögren's syn-
  drome

Familial factors, 38-42
  in children, 198-99
Fatigue, 11, 13, 14, 185-88
  in drug-induced lupus, 151
Fats in diet, 168-69
Feldene, 167, 172
Fifth disease, 35
Flares, 69-70
  and pregnancy, 134, 139
Flu, 92, 204-5
Fluoride and osteoporosis,
  117-18
Folic acid, 139
Folk remedies, 217
Food and Drug Administration
  (FDA), 117, 140, 156, 158,

159, 161, 166, 179, 204, 205, 206
breast implants information line, 160
Foods, 167-70, 172
Fractures. *See* Osteoporosis

Genetic factors, 38-42
and lupus-like syndrome, 153-54
Geographic variations in SSPE, MS, 52-53
German measles. *See* Rubella
Glomeruli, glomerulonephritis. *See* Kidney disease
Glucocorticoids. *See* Corticosteroids
Graft, kidney, 102-5
Graves' disease, 2, 55

Hair colorings, 166, 174
Hair loss, 14, 30
postpartum (apparent), 143
Harvard University, 54
Heart block, congenital, 146-47
Heart involvement. *See* Heart block; Libman-Sacks endocarditis; Pericarditis
Helper cells. *See* T-cells
Hematologic abnormalities, 26-27
Hemodialysis, 102
Hemolytic anemia, 94
Hemorrhage, 13, 26, 27, 94, 136
Heparin, 141
Heredity. *See* Genetic factors
Herpesviruses, 46, 53, 98-99

Hip replacement, 97
Hispanics, 42
HIV (human immunodeficiency virus). *See* AIDS
HLA, 40-42, 103-4, 153
Hormone therapy, experimental, 215-16
Hormones, 43-44. *See also* Calcitonin; Estrogens
Horton, Roberta, 220-21
Hospital for Special Surgery, 220
Hospitalization rate, 3
HTLV, 48, 53
Hydralazine, hydrazine, 152, 154, 155, 166, 173
Hydrochlorothiazide, 173
Hydroxychloroquine, 75, 76, 78
Hypertension, 99
and calcium, 112
and pregnancy, 140

Ibuprofen, 78, 80
Immune complexes, 33
Immune system, 1-2
Immunizations, 92, 177-79
childhood schedule, 202-4
flu, 92, 205
measles, 51
MMR, 52
pneumonia, 92, 95
rubella, 52
Immunoglobulins, 48
Immunologic abnormalities, 27-30
in relatives, 39
Immunosuppressants, 80-82, 202
and pregnancy, 144

Imuran, 81
Indomethacin, 91
Influenza. *See* Flu
Interferon, 48
Irradiation, total lymphoid, 213-14
ITP (immune thrombocytopenia), 94
IUDs (intrauterine devices), 148

"Jan," 14-15, 24-25, 30, 56, 69, 91, 167, 187, 190, 221, 222
Johns Hopkins University, 95, 107, 133-34
Joint disease. *See* Arthritis; Osteonecrosis
Joint pain, 10, 14-15, 24-25, 35
in drug-induced lupus, 151
and sexual activity, 180-81
*See also* Arthritis
Joint surgery, 97

Kidney biopsy, 101-2
Kidney disease, 26, 90-91, 99-105
and pregnancy, 134
Kidney stones, 115
Kidney transplant, 102-5
Knee replacement, 97

La (nuclear antigen), 32, 41, 146, 147, 151, 176
Laboratory tests, value of, 64, 74
LAC. *See* Lupus anticoagulant
*Lancet, The,* 57
Latex fixation test, 33
LE cell, 27-28
Leukopenia, 26

Libman-Sacks endocarditis, 174-75
Life expectancy. *See* Survival rates
Light sensitivity. *See* Photosensitivity
Lipids, 78, 170
"Lisa," 15-16, 23-24, 69, 76, 89, 97, 98, 171, 221, 222
Lovastatin, 152
Lumbar puncture, 26
Lupus anticoagulant, 32-33, 136-37
Lupus Foundation of America, 61, 221, 222-30
Lupus, origin of name, 6-7
Lupus-like syndromes, 149-63
LupusLine, 220-21
Lymphokines, 48
Lymphotropic viruses, 48

Magnetic resonance imaging, 96
Mammography, 68, 161, 162
Maryland State Health Department, 140
McGill University, 217
Measles
immunization, 51
and SSPE, 51-52
virus, 46
Medications, 73-92
for children, 201
and lupus-like syndrome, 152-54
and photosensitivity, 172-73
in pregnancy and breast-feeding, 143-45

Menopause, 43, 107, 108, 110, 181-83
Mentor Corporation, 160
Methylprednisolone (Medrol), 88, 91
Mevacor, 152
MHC, 40-42
Mice (research "models"), 44, 154, 168, 215, 216
Miscarriage. *See* Pregnancy
Misinformation, 3-5, 37-38
MMR vaccine, 52
Monoclonal antibodies, 214-15
Motrin, 78, 80
Mouth dryness. *See* Sjögren's syndrome
Mouth sores. *See* Oral lesions
MRI. *See* Magnetic resonance imaging
Multiple sclerosis, 39, 52-53
Mumps virus, 46
Mycoplasmas, 54
Myxoviruses, 46, 53

"Nancy," 16-17, 30, 69, 71, 82, 90-91, 187, 189
Naproxen (Naprosyn), 80
National Academy of Sciences, 111
National Cancer Institute information service, 162
National Institutes of Health (NIH), 81, 111, 112
Native Americans, 42
Necrosis. *See* Osteonecrosis
Neonatal lupus, 146-47

Nephritis, nephrosis, nephrotic syndrome. *See* Kidney disease
Neural-tube defects, 139
New York Hospital-Cornell Medical Center, 115, 220
New York University Medical Center, 147, 170
Nifedipine, 83
Nolvadex, 183
Nonsteroidal anti-inflammatory drugs. *See* NSAIDs
Norplant, 148
nRNP, 32, 174
NSAIDs, 78-80, 167
Number of persons with lupus, 2
Nuprin, 78
Nutrition Information Center, 115

O'Connor, Flannery, 25n
Oral contraceptives, 11, 147-48, 152
Oral lesions, 11, 15, 180
Osteonecrosis, 95-98, 201
    and sexual activity, 180
Osteoporosis, 91, 107-31, 181-82

Pamidronate, 117
Pap tests (smears), 68, 175
Parainfluenza viruses, 46
Paramyxoviruses, 46, 53
Parvovirus, 35
Pasteur Institute (Paris), 49
Pericarditis, 25-26
Pets. *See* Animals

Phagocytes, phagocytosis, 27-28, 33
Phlebitis, 11
Photosensitivity, 23-24, 54, 83-84, 170-73
  in children, 201-2
Physician-patient relationship, 59-72
Piroxicam, 167, 172
Plaquenil, 75, 91
Plasmapheresis, 211-13
Pleurisy, pleuritis, 10, 25-26
Pneumonia, 92, 95
Polyarthritis, 13
Poxviruses, 46
Pravastatin, 153
Prayer, 193-94
Prednisolone, 88
Prednisone, 87-88, 91, 94
  and pregnancy, 140, 141
Preeclampsia, 141-42
Pregnancy, 11, 133-48
  antimalarials in, 76
  and calcium, 112
President's Council on Physical Fitness, 120
Prevalence of lupus, 2-3
Procainamide (Procan, Pronestyl), 152, 154
Procardia, 83
Prolactin, 216
Proteinuria, 26
  and pregnancy, 141
Psoralens, 172
Psychiatric problems and corticosteroids, 90n

Psychological aspects. See Emotional factors
Psychotherapy. See Counseling
PTT (partial thromboplastin time), 33, 136
Public Health Service, 139
Pulmonary emboli, 11
Pulse therapy, 81

Quinacrine, 75, 76
Quinine derivatives. See Antimalarials

Racial distribution, 42
Ranitidine, 79
Rashes, 15-16, 35, 199. See also Butterfly rash; Skin lesions
Raynaud's phenomenon, 16, 30-31, 32, 82-83, 95
  and breast implants, 157, 158
  and sexual activity, 180
Remodeling of bone, 109
Renal disease. See Kidney disease
Reoviruses, 46
Rest, 185-88
Retroviruses, 47-50, 53
Reverse transcriptase, 48
Reye's syndrome, 204
Rheumatic fever, 200
Rheumatoid arthritis, 10, 28, 29, 33, 39, 41, 78
Rheumatoid factor, 33-34
Rheumatologists, rheumatology, 60, 68, 201
RNA viruses, 46-50
Ro, 32, 41, 146, 147, 151, 176

Rollin, Betty, 162
Roseola virus (HHV-6), 46
Rubella, 46, 52

S.L.E. Foundation, 220
Salicylates, 78-79, 80
Saline breast implants, 161,
    162-63
Salsalate, 79
Sed rate, 31
Seizures, 26
Sensitivity in diagnostic testing,
    21-22. See also Allergies;
    Photosensitivity
Sex ratios of patients, 3, 42-45,
    198
Sexual activity, 177, 179-81
Shanghai Medical University,
    217
Shingles, 53, 98-99
Sicca syndrome. See Sjögren's
    syndrome
Side effects. See specific medica-
    tions
Silicone gel breast implants,
    155-63, 166-67
Simvastatin, 153
Sjögren's syndrome, 32, 49, 147,
    175-77
    and breast implants, 156, 157,
        158
    and sexual activity, 180
Skin lesions, 2, 23, 199. See also
    Butterfly rash; Discoid
    lesions; Rashes
Slow viruses, 51-52
Sm, 28, 32, 41

Smoking, 166
    and osteoporosis, 108, 110
    and pregnancy, 138
    and Raynaud's, 82
Southern Medical Journal, 194
Specialties, medical, 60
Specificity, 21-22
Spinal tap, 26
Splenectomy, 94, 95
Spontaneous abortion. See
    Pregnancy
SSPE, 51-52
Stanford University, 214
Steroids. See Corticosteroids
Stress, 69-70
Sulfa drugs, 152, 173
Sulindac, 80, 86
Sun sensitivity. See Photosensi-
    tivity
Sunscreens, 171-72
Super-antigens, 50
Support groups, 219-30
Suppressor cells. See T-cells
Surgery
    for contraception, 148
    joint, 97
    kidney, 101 (biopsy), 102-5
        (transplant)
    tendon, 98
Survival rates, 4-5, 202
Symptoms, 20
    in children, 199
    in women vs. men, 44-45
Syphilis, false-positive test for,
    12, 27, 32, 135

T-cells, 48, 49-50

Tagamet, 79
Tai chi, 193
Tamoxifen, 183, 215-16
Tartrazine, 166, 173
Teeth. *See* Dental care
Tendon rupture, 97, 98
Tetracyclines, 54, 172
Thrombocytes, 94
Thrombocytopenia, 26, 27, 94, 136
Thrombophlebitis, 11
Thyroid disease, 2, 39
Tolmetin (Tolectin), 80
Total lymphoid irradiation, 213-14
Toxemia of pregnancy. *See* Preeclampsia
Toxic shock syndrome, 50
Transplant, kidney, 102-5
Travel, 178-79, 186
Tripterygium, 217-18
Tubal ligation, 148
Tuberculosis and corticosteroids, 90
Tuberculosis, cutaneous, 6-7
Twins and lupus, 39-40, 198

Ulcers. *See* Oral lesions
Ultraviolet light, 172. *See also* Photosensitivity
United Network for Organ Sharing (UNOS), 103
University of California, 218
University of California, Davis, 160
University of California, Los Angeles (UCLA), 157

University of California, San Francisco, 194
University of Connecticut, 95
University of Maryland, 107
University of South Florida, 157
University of Texas, 49
Uremia, 100
Urinalysis, 26

Vaccinations. *See* Immunizations
Vaginal dryness, 177
Varicella. *See* Chickenpox
Varicella-zoster virus (VZV), 46, 99
Vasculitis, 11
Vasospasm, 31, 82
Vegetarian diet, 167, 168
Verrucous endocarditis. *See* Libman-Sacks endocarditis
Viruses, 45-54
Vitamin D, 109, 114
Vitamin supplements, 169-70
von Hebra, Ferdinand, 7
VZIG (varicella-zoster immune globulin), 205-6
VZV. *See* Varicella-zoster virus

Western blot, 34
Working out. *See* Exercise

X-linked disorders, 42-43
Xerostomia, 176

Zantac, 79
Zovirax, 99, 206

# About the Authors

**Sheldon Paul Blau, M.D.,** practices in Long Island, New York, and is clinical professor of medicine at the School of Medicine, State University of New York at Stony Brook; he is also an attending physician at Winthrop University Hospital and a consultant in rheumatology to Mercy Hospital, Long Beach Hospital, and Massapequa General Hospital. He served as chief of the Division of Rheumatic Diseases at Nassau County Medical Center from 1973 to 1990. A Fellow of the American College of Physicians and the American College of Rheumatology (formerly the American Rheumatism Association), he has served on the medical advisory boards of the Long Island/ Queens chapter of the Lupus Foundation of America and the Scleroderma Society of Greater New York.

Dr. Blau and Ms. Schultz previously co-authored *Arthritis: Complete, Up-to-Date Facts for Patients and Their Families* and *Lupus: The Body Against Itself.* Dr. Blau is also editor and co-author of the medical text *Emergencies in Rheumatoid Arthritis* and has published extensively in professional journals.

**Dodi Schultz,** an award-winning science writer, is a contributing editor of *Parents* magazine and has written for many of the other major consumer periodicals. In addition to the titles mentioned above, she is author, co-author, or editor of eighteen other books, including *The First Five Years, The Headache Book,* and *The Mothers' and Fathers' Medical Encyclopedia.* Ms. Schultz is a member of the Authors Guild, the National Association of Science Writers, and the Society of Professional Journalists and is a board member and past president of the American Society of Journalists and Authors.